18 Buddha Hands

Principles, Fundamentals, Strategy,
and Tactics of Jook Lum Temple Boxing

chinamantis.com

5 Volumes
10 Years Ongoing Research
China Southern Praying Mantis Kungfu Survey™

Volume 1
Pingshan Mantis Celebration

Volume 2
China Mantis Reunion

Volume 3
Kwongsai / Iron Ox Interviews

Volume 4
On Monk Som Dot's Trail

Volume 5
Chu Gar Mantis Celebrations

Also available!
5 volumes in one multimedia eBook!

手佛　八十　螂螳　家客

Eighteen Buddha Hands

Principles, Fundamentals, Strategy, and Tactics of Jook Lum Temple Boxing

Featuring
Late Sifu Louie Jack Man

by

Roger D. Hagood

Charles Alan Clemens, Editor

Southern Mantis Press　|　Pingshan Town, China

southernmantispress.com

Copyright © 2012 by Roger D. Hagood

All rights reserved. No part of this publication may be reproduced, distributed, or transmitted in any form or by any means, including photocopying, recording, or other electronic or mechanical methods, without the prior written permission of the publisher, except in the case of brief quotations embodied in critical reviews and certain other noncommercial uses permitted by copyright law. For permission requests, email to the publisher, addressed "Attention: Permissions Coordinator," at the address below.

Southern Mantis Press
462 W. Virginia St. (Rt. 14)
Crystal Lake, Illinois 60014
1-800-Jook Lum
books@southernmantispress.com

Ordering Information:
Special discounts are available for martial art schools, bookstores, specialty shops, museums and events.
Contact the publisher at the address above.

Printed in the United States of America
ISBN: 978-0-9857240-1-6

First Edition

kwongsaimantis.com

Dedication

Sifu Gin Foon Mark

In 1979, Sifu Louie Jack Man called Mark Sifu and said "I'm sending Roger to you. I've taught him all I can." In 1980, I joined Mark Sifu in Minnesota, USA and became his pupil by ceremony. In 1987, he and I travelled to Mexico and promoted Kwongsai Mantis on Mexican national television. We talk monthly these days and Mark Sifu has asked me to write a book for him. I hope it will be possible soon. Sifu's teaching was genius and he didn't train kungfu, he was kungfu. --- RDH

somdotmantis.com

Monk Som Dot's Ancestral Shrine

**Kwongsai Jook Lum Temple
Praying Mantis Kungfu**

Hoc Yurn; Hoc Yi; Hoc Kungfu

學仁　學義　學功夫

Jurn Jow; Jurn Si; Jurn Gow Do

尊祖　尊師　尊道義

Respect the Ancestors for their transmission of the art.

Respect the Sifu for his teaching.

Respect the Older Brothers for their dedication and loyalty.

Respect the Younger Brothers for determination in training.

Contents

Preface xii

From Whence We Came: Origins

- Kwongsai—Jiangxi on the map 2
- Mount Dragon Tiger 4
- Jook Lum Temples in China 5
- Monk Som Dot gives birth to a Pai 6
- Lam Sang plants Mantis in the USA 9
- Kungfu Master Gin Foon Mark 18
- Louie Jack Man Sifu 19

About the Kungfu: Principles

- Hsing-Ming Kung: The Foundation of All Kungfu 23
- Song of the Body Posture and Stance 36
- Rooting, Centering 41; Spiral Power 44
- Centerline Principle (Inner / Outer gate) (12-6; 3-9) 46
- Contact, Control, Strike — One Arm-Three Hands 48
- Intercepting and Sticky Hand 49
- Single - Double Bridge; Anticipating - Telegraphing 50
- Dead and Live Power—Lik and Ging Power 51
- Form and Function 53
- 3 Methods of Bridging: Crushing; Swallowing; Evading 56
- Float; Sink; Swallow; Spit 57
- Internal Training 58
- Da Mak - Dim Mak Vital Point Striking 62   108   67

ironoxmantis.com

Contents

About the Kungfu: Fundamentals

Footwork

- Opening the Horse **75**; Shuffle Step **75**
- Turnarounds Back and Front **76**; Chop Step **76**
- Circle Step **77**; Advance Step **77**
- Return Steps **78**; Chop, Circle, Advance as One **78**
- Half Steps **79**; Side to Side Stepping **79**
- One, Two, Three Steps Forward **80**; List of Steps **81**
- Fundamentals Continued **81 - 83**
  Kicks, Sweeps, Takedowns, Grappling, Chin Na, Hooking Hands, Elbow Strokes, Dui Jong Two Man Strengthening, Sticky Hand Training, Single Man Forms, Two Man Forms
- Three Phases of Training **84**
  Conscious, Instinctual, Intuitive

Eighteen Buddha Hand Skills

9 Defensive Skills

- Empty Buddha Hand **86**
- Hands are a Pair of Doors **87**
- Mor Shu: The Grinding Hand **89**
  Attributes: inner–outer hooking; neutralizing; simultaneous attack and defense; defense only; defend and strike with the same hand; defend and strike with the opposite hand; inside gate—outside gate; single bridge—double bridge
- Gwak Shu: The Sweeping Hand **91**
  Attributes: defense only; defend and strike with the same

Contents

hand; defend and strike with the opposite hand; inside gate—outside gate; single bridge—double bridge

- Choc Shu: The Upper Hooking Hand 93
  Attributes: defense only; defend and strike with the same hand; defend and strike with the opposite hand; inside gate—outside gate; single bridge—double bridge

- Sai Shu: The Roller Arm 95

- Sic Shu: The Eating Hand 97

- Chun Shu: Straight Strike 99
  Simultaneous Offense & Defense

- Pak Shu: Palm Heel Strike 101

- Lop Shu: Grabbing Hand 103

- Gop Shu: Capturing Hand 105

9 Offensive Skills

- Jek (Jet) Shu: Straight Strike 107

- Bao Chong: Palm Strike 109

- Bil Jee: Exploding Finger Strikes 111

- Ping Shu: Back of the Hand Strikes 113

- Jung Shu: Uppercut 115

- Chop Shu: Finger Pokes 117

- Gow Choy: Hammer Fist 119

- Jang Shu: Elbow Strokes 121

- Han Shu: Double Bridge Strikes 123

List of Eighteen Hands 125

southmantis.com

Contents

Acknowledgements 126

Appendix A: Lam Sang's Three Generations 127
- First Generation Photograph 128
- Second Generation Photograph 129
- Masonic Association Photographs 130—132
- Three Generations—One Teaching 133

Appendix B: Miscellanies 134
- Note on Hand Names and Translations 134
- About Southern Mantis on the Internet 134
- About the Photographs in this Book 135

Appendix C: Chronology 136

Resources
- China Southern Praying Mantis Kungfu Survey™ Volumes 1—5 137—141
- MantisFlix™ Movies and Events 142
- Our Family of Websites 143
- Instructional Playing Cards 145
- Instructional DVDs 147
- Join A School—Start a Study Group 148

Author's Bio 149

Preface

In 1978, I had black belts in two different arts and basic training in several others. I had lived and studied in Hawaii and Korea. And, I was 101st Airborne US Army, stationed at Ft. Campbell, Kentucky. There were very few martial arts schools other than Tae Kwon Do in those days.

160 miles away, in search of kungfu, I made my way into a small Chinese restaurant in Bowling Green, Kentucky and found Master Louie Jack Man, head chef. I remember asking the owner of this, the only Chinese restaurant in Bowling Green at the time, if there was any Chinese Kungfu nearby.

He stated his head chef was excellent in kungfu and if I cared to wait until 10:30 that evening, he would introduce me. As a young martial artist, just 22 years old, I was always willing to try my hand at something new, and so, over several pots of oolong tea and a few dozen fortune cookies, I waited.

It was then my first teacher of Southern Praying Mantis appeared, Master Louie, smoking a cigarette, with a slightly arched back, sliding his feet as he walked across the floor. Looking rather distant, he asked, "So, you want to learn kungfu?" To which I replied, "I am a black belt."

He laughed, waved me away with the back of his hand and said, "I don't know any kungfu, sorry." It was very humbling to a young martial artist raised on TV and kungfu movies and a good lesson in etiquette.

In December 1979, Louie Sifu introduced me to his Sihing (older brother) Master Gin Foon Mark and in June, 1980, I entered Mark Sifu's school. He (Mark Sifu) was everything I expected and more out of a traditional kungfu teacher. In 1987, we travelled south of Mexico City,

Preface

Mexico, together, where we introduced Jook Lum Temple Praying Mantis Kungfu on Mexican National Television during a 10 day seminar with 120 participants.

I have always respected and supported Mark Sifu. It is primarily due to his effort that the non-Chinese public has become aware of Southern Praying Mantis. His film Kungfu Master: Gin Foon Mark is available in libraries throughout the world and was shown on HBO during the 1980s. I keep regular contact with him today still and he has asked me several times to write a book for him. He is still going strong at 84 and this book is dedicated to him and the memory of Louie Sifu.

Even in 1978, Louie always called Mark "dai Sihing or big brother" of Mantis and said Mark Sifu was number one! He said if one calls him Master then he must call Gin Foon Mark Grandmaster. He states that Master Mark and his partner, Chen Ho Dun, were instrumental to him and the other members of Chinese Freemasons learning and practicing Mantis in the 60s.

Louie Sifu passed in 2011. He was 80. He was always open, friendly, honest and kind. I often went to see him in Philadelphia Chinatown. He came to my school and taught my students. In the late 1970s and early 1980s , I accompanied him to demonstrate Jook Lum during the Chinese New Year Celebrations in Atlanta, Georgia. I also travelled with him to New York City, New York and Atlantic City, New Jersey several times on Mantis visits to Lam Sang's Pai.

Louie Sifu was keenly family oriented. He loved his family dearly and I often saw him

Preface

forego what he wanted to do just to stay near and care for his family. He worked as a chef seven days a week for years. He loved to cook and his cuisine was five star. If I visited him at the restaurants while he was working, I never had to order from the menu. He would always cook and send out his most delectable dishes like real bird's nest soup, orange beef, and seafoods of many types. He knew what I liked and he enjoyed watching me enjoy his meals, although, he rarely ate anything. He didn't eat much at any meal. He enjoyed his cigarettes and tea and I enjoyed bringing those to him anytime I saw him.

One day, he asked me, "Lets go?" I asked, "Where?" He just started walking down the streets of Philly Chinatown with me in tow. He chatted with everyone, stopping by the fire station, several shops and people on the street. We ended up at a typical Chinatown shop quite far away. The owner was a Sifu and friend of his. Sifu told the owner we wanted a Sun Toi, Ancestral Shine, and the owner quickly dispatched two female clerks to retrieve all the necessary items. I had not asked Sifu to transmit a shrine to me and it was a surprise. Sifu then asked an old calligrapher friend to write the couplets. I paid for the shrine artifacts and offered to give Sifu a red envelope but he didn't want it. He just said, "From this time, do whatever you want in Mantis, but stick with the traditional transmission."

During the 1990s and even up to his passing he continued to promote and teach. We kept in contact regularly from that first day we met in 1978, when he laughingly waved me away with the back of his hand.

RDH
Pingshan Town
Guangdong, China
Summer, 2012

From Whence We Came: Origins

Kwongsai On the Map

Hakka Roots of Southern Mantis in Jiangxi Province

Kwongsai (gong[1] sai[1]) is a romanization of the Cantonese pronunciation for Jiangxi province, China.

Located in the middle reaches of the Yangtze River in southeast China, Jiangxi is home to some 45 million people, mostly Han Chinese. Other ethnic groups include the Huizu, Miaozu, Yaozu, and Hakka. It is subtropical with hot, humid summers and cold winters.

Lushan Mountain, located in northern Jiangxi, is listed as one of the world cultural heritages in China. And nearby Poyang Lake, the largest fresh water lake in China, is a kingdom of rare birds

2

Eighteen Buddha Hands

and animals. And Jiangxi also has many ancient and sacred places such as Dragon Tiger Mountain, which is a sacred Taoist shrine and the abode of the ancient Taoist Popes.

Jiangxi was ruled by various dynasties from as early as 770 BC. There was an extended period of peace during the Ching Dynasty (1644-1911), which ended in revolution. Warlord rule continued until Chiang Kai-shek and the Nationalists achieved control of the province in 1926. Jiangxi was under Japanese occupation from 1938 to 1945. Communist forces took control in 1949.

It is said the Fujian Shaolin Ancestors Lee Shik Hoi and Lam Wing Chui went to Jiangxi, circa 1703, and established the fifth Shaolin Triad Lodge known as the "Extensive Conversion Hall of the Western Dyke District." Its flag was green with the character "together." Therefore similarities in Jiangxi's indigenous Kungfu was early on influenced by Fujian Shaolin and styles with a similar "root" can be found in the neighboring provinces, especially Fujian - Guangdong.

From Whence We Came

Dragon Tiger Mountain

Southern Praying Mantis Kungfu is said to have originated by monk Som Dot, in the bamboo forests of Mt. Dragon-Tiger, Jiangxi province. The scenic mountain range resembles a dragon and tiger bowing to each other and is located 12 miles southwest of Yingtan city. Because of its beautiful mountains and valleys it has been called the capital of spirits and a living place of gods. From the mountain top, 99 peaks offer scenic vistas up to six miles in the distance—a wonder of natural beauty.

The first Taoist Pope of China, Zhang Dao Ling, established his religious authority there which continued through sixty three unbroken generations on Dragon Tiger Mountain until 1949.

From his Taoist influence of magic and charms evolved a mystical element in kungfu, including Southern Praying Mantis, known as 'shen kung' or spirit power kungfu. Initially a practitioner may be involved in 49 days of asceticism which results in his being protected from the spirit world as well as from all earthly adversaries.

During a ceremony in front of a school's ancestral tablet or altar, the master asks the kungfu ancestors to enter the disciple's body. Using a red cloth and magical spells, the disciple is then instructed to sleep before the altar for

江西龍虎山竹林寺螳螂派

seven weeks in which time his soul will pass through the underworld of evil spirits eventually to be reborn as a member of the new 'spiritual kungfu' group.

The function of such practice was to boost the warrior-disciple's confidence and to foment an undaunted spirit which could deal with and survive any matter at hand.

China Jook Lum Temples with Southern Praying Mantis

Wu Tai Shan—Five Peaks Mountain—Shanxi Province
The oldest Bamboo Forest Temple has Som Dot Manuscripts

Long Hu Shan—Dragon Tiger Mt.—Jiangxi Province
Once set among the splendor of the Taoist Pope's palaces;
Jook Lum Temple non-existent today

Hong Kong Jook Lum Temple
A beautiful large complex but without Som Dot's Shaolin Order

Macau Jook Lum Temple
Claims Lee Siem as their 'Patron Saint of Kungfu'

Monk Som Dot Gives Birth To Southern Praying Mantis

It is said that Monk Som Dot was originally from Tibet and that he wandered extensively studying Shaolin boxing and medicine.

At the invitation of the Taoist Pope he travelled to Kwongsai Mt. Dragon Tiger and after settling there, he accepted two disciples, Wong Leng, an illiterate, but diligent disciple, and Lee Siem. Lee Siem later became known as Siem Yuen, which means capable of grasping the depth of Buddhism. And Wong Leng became known as Wong Do Yuen, capable in Taoism.

After some years, Som Dot sent his two disciples down the mountain to spread his art of Shaolin, which was divided into three orders. The first order taught the principle of 10 soft and one hard, and was taught only on the top of the mountain. The second order was half hard, half soft power. The third order was based on extremely forceful techniques. This is the reason the art is sometimes called a "three door or gate" art today.

In doing so, as they descended the mountain, Wong Do Yuen and Lee Siem Yuen, at the middle gate of the mountain accepted a student named Chu Long Bot. Hiding the kungfu of the first order, they taught Chu Long Bot only the second order kungfu of Som Dot. At that time, the first order kungfu of Som Dot was not taught.

After learning the art, Chu, having no knowledge of the first order kungfu, betrayed Wong and Lee and used only the Chu surname to pass on what became 'Chu Gar Gao' - Chu Family Creed. The name was later changed again to "Chu Gar Praying Mantis" in Hong Kong.

Chu Long Bot later taught Chu An Nam, who taught Yang Sao and Lao Sui, who was a friend of Chu Kwei, who was the father of Chu Kwong Hua in contemporary times. This order of kungfu was originally taught only at the middle gate of the mountain.

Later, as Wong Do Yuen and Lee Siem Yuen went back down the mountain, at the lower gate, a praying mantis insect popped out in front of them. Wong, being the first to step off the mountain, proclaimed the mantis must be a sign from Heaven and to avoid further persecution of Som Dot's Shaolin teaching, the Shaolin art of three orders should simply be called Praying Mantis.

At the bottom of the mountain, a man surnamed Choy and nicknamed Tit Ngau, or Iron Ox, pleaded with sincerity to learn their kungfu and the two of them taught him Som Dot's third order of kungfu based on extremely forceful techniques.

Not knowing what to call the art, Choy, having no knowledge of the first or second order of Som Dot, eventually did the same as the Chu Clan and called the art Tit Ngau, or Iron Ox. Later a fellow named Chung Lo Ku learned from Choy and passed on this teaching as Chung Gar Gao in the East River region. This kungfu of the third order was taught at the bottom of the mountain.

In China, it is said each of Som Dot's three orders of Shaolin Kungfu has its advantage and each is worthwhile to learn and study.

Author's note: For an in-depth look at the origins and history of Southern Praying Mantis in China refer to the book, Pingshan Mantis Celebration, also from SouthernMantisPress.com. Also, refer to the five volume eBook, China Southern Praying Mantis Kung Survey™ at chinamantis.com. (Monk Images are representations only.)

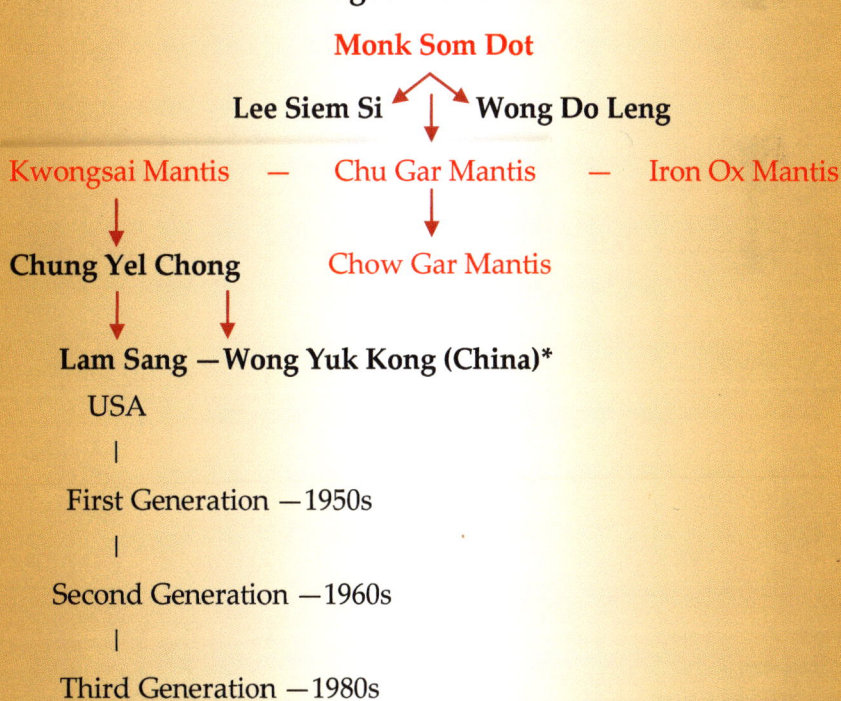

Abridged Transmission

Monk Som Dot

Lee Siem Si ← ↓ → **Wong Do Leng**

Kwongsai Mantis — Chu Gar Mantis — Iron Ox Mantis

↓ ↓

Chung Yel Chong   Chow Gar Mantis

↓ ↓

Lam Sang — **Wong Yuk Kong (China)***

USA
|
First Generation — 1950s
|
Second Generation — 1960s
|
Third Generation — 1980s

*refer to **Pingshan Mantis Celebration** in Hardcover

Eighteen Buddha Hands

Monkey, the Grand Teacher, plants Kwongsai Mantis in the USA
Late Lam Wing Fay (1910—1981)

Lam Sang planted a seed of Kwongsai Mantis in the USA as early as the late 1940s. The seed continues to blossom today, and his teaching has only slightly changed through his three generations of disciples over the last sixty years.

When Lam Sifu, being Hakka himself, first arrived in New York City, he went straight to the "Sun Jing Hui" Hakka Chinese Association.

As was customary at the Association, people played Chinese checkers and mahjong passing the days away sipping tea and socializing. Lam was a small man, barely five foot tall, and sitting on a bar stool with legs crossed smoking a big cigar, he was approached by Uncle Chen, the Hakka Association kungfu teacher.

Uncle Chen, already aged a bit, said to Lam Sang, "You look like a little monkey sitting here with your legs crossed smoking that big cigar." Lam Sang replied, "Would you care to give me a try?" Uncle Chen (perhaps thinking it would be a piece of cake) said, "If I can't pass your hand then I will carry your suitcases for the rest of my life."

A bout ensued and Uncle Chen was squarely defeated then and there on the spot. True to his word, Uncle Chen until the day he died, did follow Lam Sang carrying his bags.

He (Uncle Chen) even trained a bit of Kwongsai Mantis. Lam Sifu's first generation of disciples who lived in the same apartment with him said that Uncle Chen learned only Mor Sao but could using that easily throw them up against the wall. It was only after Lam's disciples spent a longer time and learned more that Uncle Chen could no longer control them.

Lam Sang, sitting on a bar stool, smoking a big cigar, resembled a little monkey. After he defeated Uncle Chen in that bout, the nickname "Monkey" stuck to him and henceforth, he was known as "Monkey."

Even today, most over 60 in NYC Chinatown have stories of a reserved man of small stature able to perform supernormal feats of strength. Few are the masters of old today!

Note: Lam Sifu's t-shirt states "Kun Ying Hui" which means "a gathering of heroes."

Lam Sang—A Brief History

In the late 1920s, Lam became a disciple of Master Chung Yel Chong in Pingshan Town, Guangdong, China. After several years of living with Master Chung, Lam decided he had trained enough to leave.

At the time the Chung family lived 'three generations under one roof' and Master Chung's mother was a kungfu master in her own right. At that time kungfu women travelled from village to village demonstrating and learning kungfu. They were respected as fighting women.

Although Lam Sang decided he had enough training, Master Chung's mother had other ideas. As he tried to leave, she stood in the gate. She said only if the young Lam could pass her

三達門中傳妙手

江西竹林寺螳螂派

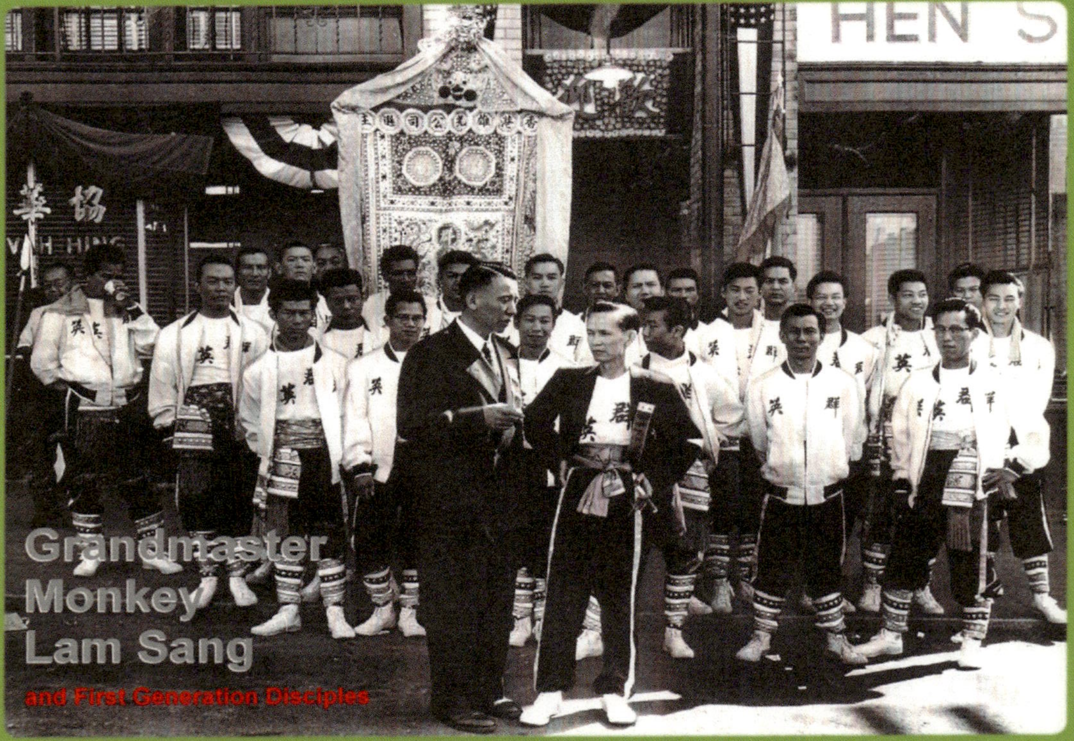

Grandmaster Monkey Lam Sang and First Generation Disciples

竹林寺內煉精功

From Whence We Came

hands, could he then leave. Try as he might, he could not and she stayed his departure only to add further to his kungfu training. Some have said it was she who introduced monkey stepping to the Kwongsai Southern Praying Mantis style.

At a later time when he did leave, it is said that the young Lam accompanied his grand teacher, the Monk Lee Siem, for a number of years to the Jook Lum Temple and there he learned all the skills of Som Dot's mantis style as well as a number of special skills such as Lee Siem's double short swords and straight sword.

During the second world war, Lam Sang had joined a Hong Kong organization to fight against the Japanese invasion of China. He taught many students and his efforts against the Japanese oppression were considered outstanding. Toward the last years of the war, at the insistence of Lee Siem, he took the teachings of Som Dot to England. It is said some in Liverpool still train his kungfu. Leaving the UK, he finally settled in Chinatown, New York City, USA where he taught hundreds of students and a handful of disciples at three Associations; Sun Jing Hui Hakka Association, Hip Sing Tong and the Chinese Freemason Club.

During a period of retirement beginning in the late 1960s Grandmaster Lam travelled to Indonesia, Thailand, India and Taiwan. He finally returned back to the USA in 1981 and settled in Chinatown again.

If the meaning of Grandmaster is simply "one who has trained Masters" then Lam Sang was Grandmaster of Kwongsai Mantis in the USA. Passing in 1991, he was survived by two sons and a daughter and had hundreds of students, grand students and disciples. He was self-disciplined, hard working and humble. It is said his students respected him and he loved them very much.

Photo left: Wednesday, September 10, 1958, Seattle Times Newspaper; Ancient Rituals Performed in Chinatown. Ceremonial dancers performed ancient rituals in Seattle's Chinatown today as delegates gathered for the 40th annual convention of the Hip Sing Association. The Association is the largest Chinese fraternal organization in the United States with 25,000 members. (Lam Sang, disciples and students)

Eighteen Buddha Hands

Stories of a Supernatural Lam

Monkey was a Horse King

First generation disciples say Lam Sifu could have all his pockets stuffed with cash in the morning but return at night completely broke. His favorite pastime was horse racing and he always sat in the same seat at the race track. One day he put his newspaper down in his seat and went to buy a ticket. Upon returning there were three sailors sitting there and one in Lam's chair. He asked the sailor to get up and explained that was his lucky chair and he always sat there.

But, the sailors looked down on this little Chinese man and standing up in confrontation ordered him to leave! Lam is said to have used the 18 point technique of attacking with fingertips the bladder in a downward motion which caused one of the sailors to slump back in the chair and urinate on himself! He soon recovered and they let Lam Sifu have his seat back!

Poison Snake Staff

Once there was a Sifu of another southern style who barricaded the door of one of the Chinese Associations preventing Lam Sifu from entry. Using a large heavy wooden staff he challenged Lam Sang to try to get inside. Lam retrieved a staff and when that Sifu struck hard at Lam's head it is said that Lam used the poison snake staff with vibrating "ging" power and in only one defense and simultaneous counter strike caused the other Sifu to drop the staff from his bleeding palms. Like holding a baseball bat tight and banging it against a telephone pole the reverberations are painful!

Lam Sang is Hakka from Pingshan Town

Iron Uncle Chung Wu Xing was born in 1907 and never left Pingshan. He was about 97 when he passed a few years ago. He stated during the 1920s, Chung Yel Chong opened his first

From Whence We Came

Iron Uncle Chung Wu Xing, aged 95

Kwongsai Mantis Tong in Pingshan Town, the Shang Mo Tong, Highest Martial Hall, and accepted students including Lam Sang and Wong Yuk Kong.

Uncle Chung said they all recreated together in the Pingshan opium dens back in those days. He also said that Lam Wing Fei (Lam Sang) had a brother named Lam Choy who later on opened a bookstore in Taiwan.

According to Iron Uncle Chung, Chung Yel Chong's family and Lam Sang's family, early on, resided on opposite sides of the street in the Ma Sai area of Pingshan. Today, the "Dai Wong Yea" area where all the "Lams" and "Chungs" resided, is a football field and the old houses are torn down. Iron Uncle Chung also said that he, Lam Sang and Chung Yel Chong often went to Quarry Bay in Hong Kong in the 30s where they smoked in the opium dens and recreated together.

Macau Jook Lum Temple

Lam Sang accompanied his teacher Chung Yel Chong to visit Lee Siem (second generation ancestor) on Lee's 80th birthday. It is said that Lee Siem celebrated his 80th birthday in the Macau Jook Lum Temple where he received Chung Yel Chong and his student Lam Wing Fei (Lam Sang). It seems that Lee Siem's given name when born in 1863 was Li Guan Qing, and his Buddhist names were Lee Siem Yuen (capable of grasping truth) and Lee Chan Shi (Buddhist Master). When I questioned those in attendance at this Temple circa 2002, I was asked to wait a moment

Macau Jook Lum Temple is hidden in a busy residential area and surrounded by bamboo

with patience while a senior was rounded up. When I asked the senior about Som Dot and Lee Siem, he promptly stated that "Lee Siem is this Temple's patron Saint of Kungfu."

There was a record of Lam and Chung visiting Lee Siem at the Macau Temple in 1943.

Two primary reasons exist as to why Lam Sang's teaching differs (in name) from the Kwongsai Mantis in China; first is that Lam Sang was very private to the point of secrecy and so not many today have seen or understand his original teaching and secondly it is said that Lam travelled with monk Lee Siem who taught him the separate skills he passed on in New York City. Some today say that Lam mixed his teaching with this or that or that he learned Chu Gar, that he was never a student of Chung Yel Chong and more. However, the first hand evidence of Lam still exists in China today as evidenced above by the extant 1943 records at the Macau Jook Lum Temple, the family of Chung Yel Chong and the China elders still living who knew and were friends of Lam.

Fireworks, No Urination, Sky Claw

In the late 1950s, when Lam Sifu was living together in one apartment with his first generation of 7 disciples, he had a hard time to get them off the bed before daybreak. Lam resorted to throwing firecrackers under their bed and the noise and smoke aroused them to head to the roof. As part of their kungfu training they had to reach the rooftop before daylight and face toward the rising sun. There could be no urination until the "chi - vital energy" had circulated enough that the morning erection had subsided. Then without blinking they had to stare into the morning sun until tears flowed freely. Only then could they wash their face in a big pan of water. (It is said one's qigong is not cultivated unless within nine respirations one's erection subsides). And the technique of staring into the sun is called "cultivating yang energy through the eyes" or sometimes called "sky claw." Sun gazing is a popular method to unlock hidden powers in many cultures.

Lam Sang's Light Body Skill (Qing Gong)

Lam Sang Sifu was well known for his light body skills. Early on when Lam was living on Broom Street, he and three of his disciples that lived together had been to the horse track. Lam Sifu loved to bet on the horses. It was in the winter time and there was snow on the ground. One of the disciples who had won at the track that day bet his Sifu Lam $200 USD (a lot of money in those days) that he could not walk in the snow without leaving his shoe tracks!

He states that all four of them stopped and Lam Sang made a couple of movements (as if pulling up his lower dan tien) and then simply stepped again 6 or 7 steps - without leaving any sign of a track in the snow. The three disciples looked back where they came from and there were four sets of tracks - they looked forward to where Lam Sang was now standing and nothing - no tracks in the snow. They each tried going to where he was standing but the three disciples, try as they may, all left tracks in the snow.

I asked the disciple who lost the bet, "My Sibok, is that really true?" He swore several times that he saw it with his own eyes. They all saw it. And so, he paid the $200 USD to Lam Sang to his dismay and to Lam Sang's joy!

Letter from Wong Yuk Gong

In 1963, Wong Yuk Gong Sifu wrote a letter and mailed it to Lam Sang (addressed to Wong Bak Lim) in NYC. In the letter, Wong stated that one Mr. Lee had made trouble after studying with Chung Yel Chong a short time in Hong Kong and had left China perhaps to possibly arrive in NYC. Wong, addressing Lam Sang as "hing-dai", asked Lam to "close Lee down" should he attempt to open a school in NYC. Wong Included in the letter a small 2" x 2" photo of himself. There are some today who distort the facts and would demean Lam to enlarge themselves! This letter is retained today. Search and prove all things!

Lam Sifu Knows the Day of His Passing

The third generation disciples of Lam Sifu said that some days before he passed, he would don his Buddhist robes and return to his daily chanting. As his day approached he asked his disciple to prepare all things for his departure and he checked himself into the hospital and quietly passed away.

Those are first-hand stories from first-hand accounts of those who were with Lam Sifu. They are not hearsay or second-hand stories. And there are several other stories yet to be written.

Lam Sifu followed a life of "Hsing-Ming Kung" a mixture of spiritual cultivation and physical development. Most over 60 in NYC Chinatown have stories of a reserved man of small stature able to perform supernormal feats of strength. Few are those masters of old today!

Anecdote: When I made Chu Gar Mantis ceremony to Chen Ching Hong (Eugene) circa 1989 in San Francisco he repeatedly said that he had heard Lam Sang in NYC was one of excellent and perhaps supernatural skills. It was Chen Sifu who repeated a story about Lam Sang reaching into a boiling wok of oil and slowly pulling out a silver dollar. No one was sure if it was the silver protecting him, a coat of chemical oil or if he was just supernatural!

Master Gin Foon Mark

Kungfu Master Gin Foon Mark
Lam Sang 2nd Generation Circa 1960's

Mark Sifu's Promotions have made Kwongsai Jook Lum Temple Mantis Popular Worldwide!

Master Mark was born in Taishan, a city near Guangzhou, Guangdong, in 1927. He came from a family of four generations of high ranking kungfu experts. His instruction began at the age of 5 under the supervision of his uncles and grandfather. As a youth, he was introduced to a variety of styles including crane, eagle and tiger. Mark Sifu began teaching in the USA circa 1950s in New York City Chinatown. During the 60s, already teaching a variety of styles, he became a disciple of Grandmaster Lam Sang and was one of a few who graduated Master Lam's teaching. When Master Lam retired in the late 1960s to China, it was Master Mark who took up the mantle and for nearly five decades has continued promoting the Art and teaching others.

Louie Sifu, calling Master Mark older brother and number one, among many others, all say that Mark Sifu was the hardest working of Lam Sang's disciples and that Mark Sifu was one of the very few who without fail was up at 4am everyday to practice Mantis and the internal work. In addition to opening schools in NY, PA and MN, he has appeared in dozens of trade magazines, newspapers and television programs including an HBO documentary.

We cannot talk of "From Whence We Came" without speaking of Mark Sifu!

Eighteen Buddha Hands

Sifu Louie Jack Man
(1932 - 2011)

From his youth in Taishan, China, Louie Sifu was interested in martial arts. Born in 1932, times were tumultuous and world war on the horizon. China was in upheaval. In 1950, he crossed the Guangdong border into Hong Kong and took a job in the Kowloon Bus company. Rooming in the company dormitory he trained in Hung Gar, Hung Fut and White Crane along with his work mates. Then, in 1958, he moved to Philadelphia, USA and united with other family members who were already living in the USA.

From 1959, he worked in Pacific Restaurant owned by the late Chen Ho Dun's father. Chen was Mark Sifu's Mantis partner under Lam Sang. In 1960, Louie joined the Chinese Freemason Association and within a few months was asked to make formal ceremony to Lam Sang and become one of Lam's seven personal disciples during his second generation teaching. Later he made a second discipleship ceremony to learn the "Shen Kung" spirit power. Louie Sifu's martial art interest was fulfilled in Lam Sang's Mantis. In 1965, he moved back to Philadelphia but returned occasionally to visit Lam Sang in NYC before his retirement and move to Taiwan.

From Whence We Came

Outside Hammer Fist

Open Buddha Hand

Late Sifu Louie Jack Man

Louie Sifu's family were restaurateurs in Tennessee and in 1977 he moved to Kentucky and accepted work as the head chef at a small Chinese restaurant. Just a year later, in 1978, I found Louie Sifu in Bowling Green. Initially, he refused to teach but I pressed him for a month or more until he finally said, "You are going to pester me without end if I don't teach you, so come back next Sunday."

From then on, every Sunday I drove 360 miles round trip to train with Sifu. I was his first student and we trained on a tennis court at the apartment complex where he was living. I was already a trained fighter with black belts and an airborne infantry solider. Sifu said show me what you got—and then he popped me square in the face. I decided to follow the old maxim, 'if you can't beat them, join them!' His feeling hands beat my buffalo strength.

Then he moved to a big white wooden house near the restaurant in which he worked as head Chef, the House of Wan, on the Bowling Green square.

We trained in a small back room of the big white house which was crowded with a Lion Head, drum and many kinds of kungfu weapons. That was odd since Sifu didn't teach and had no students. Walk the horse, three step arrow, and tsai shu—dui jong two man exercises were the order of the day. Later 18, 108, staff, broadsword, sword and sai he shared with me.

I remember when I first saw and began to train Southern Mantis with Louie Sifu in 1978, how odd I thought it was. The short stance and short spring power seemed contrary to my Kenpo and Northern Mantis. But, I could see something different inside the kungfu and decided to stick with it. And after all, there were no kungfu schools around at that time.

Later on, Louie Sifu began teaching at a Kungfu School above the restaurant where he worked. Then, in December 1979, he introduced me to Mark Gin Foon Sifu and I moved to Minnesota. (Refer to the Preface and Dedication.)

I have always kept in touch with Louie Sifu and during one visit he and I travelled to New York to visit his teacher, Lam Sang, after Lam returned back to the USA. It was a big affair on an upper floor with more than a hundred people having dim sum in Chinatown.

In 1982, Louie Sifu moved back to Philadelphia and over the years he travelled up and down the east coast promoting and teaching mantis. He had many students since that first day I persuaded him to teach in Kentucky. In the mid 1990s he taught at the Hip Sing Chinese Association in Philadelphia and also taught at a local school.

Louie Sifu was always glad to receive others and to share his knowledge of Southern Praying Mantis. He passed in December, 2011. He is survived by his wife Kin, son Barry and daughter Shirley as well as numerous students.

His fundamental teaching continues in this book.

About the Kungfu: Principles

Intent—Warrior Spirit
The first principle is intent or will-power. Intent is simply defined as the "warrior spirit." Without it, there is no focus of the body and mind into one purpose. Strike with the soul and you will never miss. Thought and action are one.

Hsing Ming Kung

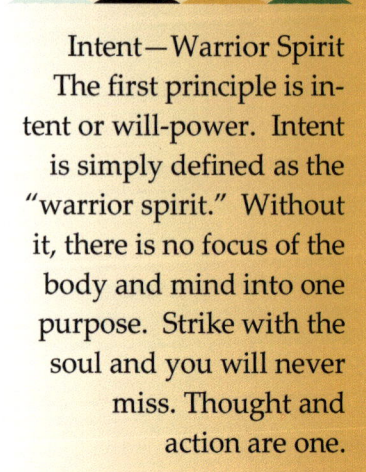

The Foundation of All Kungfu

Nei Kung Hua Shen: Changing the Character and Increasing Vitality to Purify Oneself—A short discourse by Teacher Cheng Yi Han

When beginning to undertake self cultivation (and use of higher energy) one must understand the notion of nature and life (hsing-ming). All people, however different their lives may be in other ways, are alike in this, that they possess a "natural state", an original nature. It might be likened to the portion of the light element

About the Kungfu: Principles

that is imprisoned in the darkness of the body. It is the "original nature" as it exists before it is corrupted by the contacts of life.

Before you are born, original nature can be likened to a piece of white paper, spotless. After birth, the white paper begins to be painted by the ideas of your parents and relatives and, as you grow and are swept up into the world, it is painted by the color of the world.

Again, the original nature may be likened unto a bright shiny mirror before birth. Day by day the mirror becomes covered with the dust of the world, until it no longer reflects. The purpose of self cultivation is to day after day polish the mirror of your original nature until it shines through brightly. You must erase the paint of world and family conceptions to reveal your spotless original nature. Thus it is said, "The way of the world is daily increase, but the way of cultivation is daily decrease."

As stated by Ko Hung, legendary Chinese alchemist, "If cultivators do not perform actions of merit but solely pursue the esoteric techniques, they will never attain fullness of life. Doing good stands in first place; eschewing one's faults comes next. Followers of the divine process feel that saving people in trouble so that they can avoid disaster, and protecting others from illness so that they will not die before their time, are good acts of the highest class. Loyalty, filial piety, friendliness, obedience, the human ideal, and trustworthiness are basic."

Further, it is said that to make small progress, one must do three hundred consecutive good deeds, and to make a big progress one must acquire twelve hundred good deeds. If after acquiring

Inner and Outer: Inwardly arouse the warrior spirit but outwardly appear to be calm and at peace. **Broken and Constant:** The spring power is broken into three but the warrior intent is constant.

1199, one commits a single bad deed, all the previous ones are lost, and one must begin anew. No benefit can be derived from circulating Chi energy without the accomplishment of restoring the original nature. In meditation you will reap the rewards of your good deeds.

Hence, Ming Kung and Hsing Kung are necessary to achieve results in Chi Kung. However, progress in one will lead to progress in the other. Ming Kung, the development of Righteous character in Life, will reveal the development of Original Nature. It is in meditation that the rewards of Ming Kung are brought back to the Original self. Circulation of Chi energy is the result of this natural Spiritual law. It is said that the divine process is achieved slowly and involves many taboos. It is not to be maintained without superhuman will and great energy.

The method of studying the divine processes consists of:

- A true desire to attain calm and repose, to free oneself of covetousness. To see and hear internally, and to be entranced and freed from emotion.

- Calm freedom of action, and obliviousness to our physical frames, avoiding innumerable diversions which excite the breath, heart, and mind.

- Extending Love to the things that creep and crawl, so that nothing which breathes may be harmed.

Similarity in Styles: Southern Mantis is connected by similarity with Fukien Crane, Wing Chun, Dragon, and White Eyebrow (as well as Okinawan Karate). The technique is based on a deep rooted firm upright stance, straight forward explosive force (of a sticky nature) and the use of turning and borrowing power with small deflective angles, circles and hooks.

About the Kungfu: Principles

- Regulating the breath, undergoing rituals of purification, rising with the dawn and going to sleep late in order to sublimate the five elements.

- Avoiding potent wines which trouble the harmony of the vital breath; disciplining sexual desire so that the essence is not diminished, thought processed weakened, and calm and concentration destroyed.

- Avoiding even the smell of animal flesh and purifying the intestines by stopping the intake of starches. (optional)

- Extending Love to the very frontiers of the universe and to view others as we do ourselves.

Therefore, cultivators of divine process and character travel paths different from those of the rest of mankind.

Hence, Hsing denotes man's natural constitution in which is recognized the presence of the pure, unspoiled substance connecting man's nature with the nature of the universe. Man was originally attuned with the universe and by forsaking it he did not simply infringe the spiritual law, but also severed his connection with the pure source of life. His departing from Original Nature, while constituting the greatest offense he could commit, separated him from the Way of God, and disconnects him from the whole and delivers him to himself.

Whole Body Power: For the feet, legs, and waist to act together as an integrated whole and to develop whole body power as one hand, one must keep heel-to-toe and shoulder width apart so that while advancing or withdrawing one can grasp the opportunity of favorable timing and advantageous position.

Eighteen Buddha Hands

Hsing, being the nature of man, is essentially good. Men themselves moreover, partaking all of the same nature, are "all equally men", though they may come to differ greatly from each other according to whether they pursue of neglect the essence and the ordinances of their Original Nature. Nature cannot be changed. Man, therefore, is urged to correct his subjective nature and to restore his original one.

The loss of proper nature is attributed to: the beauty of the five colors that disorder the eye; the five musical notes that disorder the ear; the five odors which disorder the dead; the five flavors which disorder the mouth; all preferences and dislikes that disorder the mind.

Hence, to restore proper nature one must remove the desires of materialism. The Original Nature will manifest as benevolence and righteousness; though the basic value of Nature is that it is originally related to Chi (life force) and Te (Virtuous Action).

Ming is destiny as decreed by Heaven. It is the appointed order of the Universe. Hsing Ming denotes the natural endowments and talents entrusted to man by Heaven and Earth. The endowments and talents of your nature are not your property. They have been appointed and made available to you that you may carry out the natural endowments and exhaust the essence. The fulfillment of one's nature, which is made possible by complying with the talents peculiar to one's constitution, will then permit the completion of his destiny as decreed by Heaven.

Physical Traits: As in any martial art, one must develop balance, timing, speed, strength and coordination. Balance from stance, timing from not being afraid to be hit, speed from repetition, strength from two man live training, and coordination from self exertion. Timing is more important than speed. The hand going out does not miss the target, coming back it brings something with it.

About the Kungfu: Principles

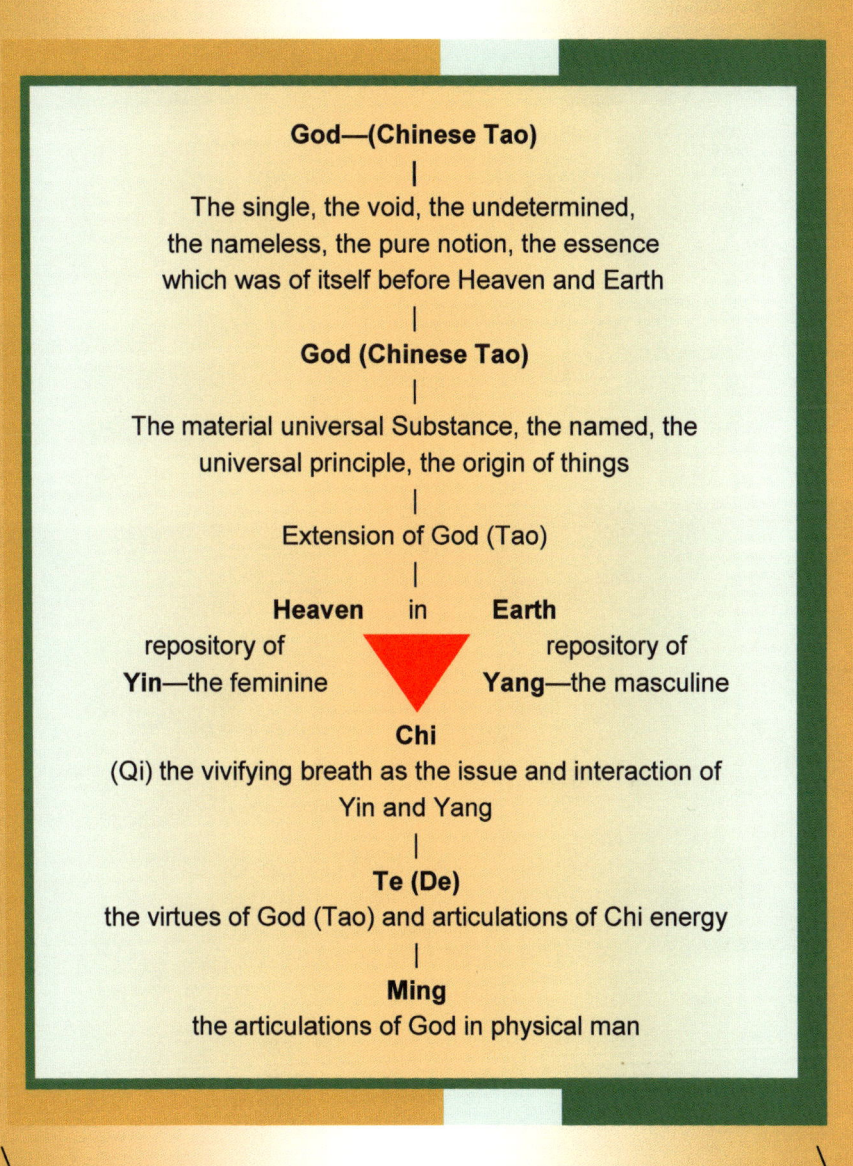

God—(Chinese Tao)

The single, the void, the undetermined, the nameless, the pure notion, the essence which was of itself before Heaven and Earth

God (Chinese Tao)

The material universal Substance, the named, the universal principle, the origin of things

Extension of God (Tao)

Heaven in **Earth**
repository of   repository of
Yin—the feminine   **Yang**—the masculine

Chi
(Qi) the vivifying breath as the issue and interaction of Yin and Yang

Te (De)
the virtues of God (Tao) and articulations of Chi energy

Ming
the articulations of God in physical man

Body Weapons: When issuing three power rooted spring force, one may employ various bodily weapons in striking; head, shoulders, elbows, forearms, wrists, fists (back fist, panther, ginger fist, phoenix, dragon, snake, thumb strikes, hammer fist), fingers, palms, hips, knees, shins, ankles, feet and toes.

Eighteen Buddha Hands

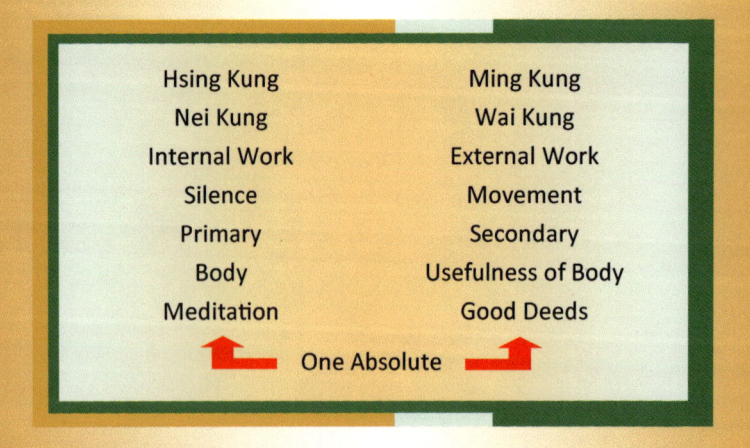

Hsing Kung	Ming Kung
Nei Kung	Wai Kung
Internal Work	External Work
Silence	Movement
Primary	Secondary
Body	Usefulness of Body
Meditation	Good Deeds

⬆ One Absolute ⬆

Meditation without Good Deeds will create (Zo Huang Lu Mo) demons.

Hsing Kung

- Repent. Body, Mind, and Spirit must be peaceful so you must meditate. Use meditation to purity the mind of no desire.

- Increase Yang energy by meditation to develop a halo which Yin energy cannot penetrate. Wrongful and bad deeds diminish the light of the body and spirit.

- Break the ego image that you have created about yourself by understanding that it is not absolute reality: you have created it.

Up and Down: If the opponent is tall, I seem taller. If the opponent is small, I seem smaller. **Forward and Back:** Advancing to me he finds the distance long. Retreating he finds the distance exasperatingly short. **Empty and Full:** Applying pressure he finds emptiness. Issuing force he cannot escape.

About the Kungfu: Principles

♦ Realize the Ego of the body ends with death.

♦ Break the gap of individuality, the Original Nature of all people is the same. The air contained inside a bottle is the same as the air outside the bottle. When the bottle is broken there is just one air. The bottle is the Body Ego and the air is the Original Nature.

♦ Consider others as yourself.

♦ Use meditation to expel the impure Chi (dzwo chi) created by negative emotion and wrongful Ming Kung (action).

Ming Kung

♦ Create good deeds and actions without thought of any reward coming to you; service to others, unselfishness, cure others illness.

♦ Take all hardship without complaint. The root of happiness is bitter hardship.

♦ The body must stop all bad habits.

♦ Cultivate a consciousness that has no temper. Anger exhausts

Hard and Soft: In training, it is very difficult to start out hard and reduce it to softness. **Sweat and Blood:** The more you sweat in training, the less you will bleed in battle. **Mercy or Cruelty:** I have a high art, I hurt with cruelty those who would damage me. - Archilocus, 650 B.C.

Eighteen Buddha Hands

the spirit's energy.

- Have a mind that is not selfish with private desires.

- Bring someone to spiritual understanding.

Hsing Kung	**Ming Kung**
Nei Yao	Wai Yao
Internal Medicine	External Medicine

Produces
Ching Dan—Golden Elixir
Sheng Tai—Spiritual Embryo

Hsing Kung	**Ming Kung**
Trigram Li	Trigram Kan
Original Nature	Subjective Nature
Fire	Water
Ching Long (Green Dragon)	Bai Hu (White Tiger)
Meditation	Good Deeds
Purification Inside Produces	Right Action Outside Returns
Right Action Outside	Original Nature Inside
Yin	Yang

Union and Harmony of **Hsing Ming** produces Chi (Vital Energy)

Mantis Tactics: A single movement of the arm may contain several actions. Tactical operations of the hand include grappling, catching, holding, capturing, clasping with the forearms, slicing strikes with the knuckles, pressing with the elbow, sudden quick pushes with both hands, spearing with extended fingers, flicking of the hands in quick jabs, exploding fingers from the fists, con't.

About the Kungfu: Principles

- Practice Hsing Kung and Ming Kung constantly.

Hsing Kung and Ming Kung cannot be separated and must be unified in sincerity.

- There is no such thing as self-cultivation with the observance of the rules of discipline.

- The most common defects of a beginner lie in his inability to lay down his habits of false thinking; of self indulgence, ignorance caused by pride and jealousy, of self inflicted obstructions caused by anger, stupidity, love, and sexual desire; of laziness and gluttony, and of attachment to wrong and right, to self and others. With a belly filled with all the above defects who can be responsive to the life force?

- Then answer this question, "If the lady Chang O came down from the moon with her naked body and embraced you in her arms, would your heart remain undisturbed; and if someone without any reason insults and beats you, will you not give rise to feelings of anger and resentment? Can you refrain from differentiating between enmity and affection, between love and hate, between self and other, between right and wrong? (A "Chan" (Zen) meditation)

- If there is awareness of purity, it becomes impurity.

Our conscience is originally pure like that of a new born baby. However, as time passes, our minds get bogged down with bad

---

Tactics, Con't: jerking the opponent's arm, slicing and chopping with the edge of the palms, hooking and deflecting hands, elbow strikes, claw-like raking actions, and poking with the back of the hands. Many of the movements are simultaneously defensive and offensive. The feet, ankles, knees, and hips may mirror the hand movements.

deeds and influences and our conscience obscured by wrong desires and insatiable wants. Man loses his character through the desire for fame, and knowledge leads to contention. In the struggle for fame, men distrust each other, while their knowledge is but an instrument for scheming and contention. Mankind is living in a "sea of sins" and treats it as though it is the "garden of happiness".

People who abnormally develop humanity, while exacting character and suppressing their nature in order to gain a reputation, make the world noisy with their discussions and cause it to follow impractical doctrine. People commit excess in arguments, like piling up bricks and tying knots, analyzing and enquiring into distinctions of hard and soft, while their identities and differences wear themselves out in vain useless terms. **In exchange for the material essentials of civilized life, man has lost certain essentials which are necessary for his peace of mind.**

The way is not far from man though it is impeded in us. He who finds it, seeks it. Man, lured by earthly attractions, is stubborn to recover his Original Nature and return to the Original State. Those who lose their selves in material things and lose their Original Nature in the material world may be compared to people who stand on their heads.

Personal Conduct in Self Cultivation

Heart

1. Honor and be obedient to parents.

Bridging, Range, Distance: A bridge is any part of the body used to close the distance to the opponent. Arms and hands are commonly the bridge. Three methods are hard bridge (smash through the opponent), soft bridge (turning or borrowing the opponent's force), and evasive bridge in which contact with the opponent is avoided or neutralized. Any and each of the, Cont'd

2. Subject to the state and loyal at heart.

3. Ready to help the poor and needy.

4. Be compassionate to those in difficulty.

5. Do not be greedy or jealous of possessions.

6. Do not harbor evil thoughts of sensual pleasure.

7. Do not be jealous of other's talent.

8. Do not blame yourself or hate others for being better.

9. Always be honest and upright.

10. In whatever you do, exercise sincerity.

Personality

1. Wear clean and neat attire. Regulate your dress carefully to show dignity and respect.

2. Perfect yourself morally and set a good example.

3. Keep your facial expression firm; walk and sit upright and straight, be respectful and well mannered, think before talking, be calm, and work according to your position.

Talking

1. Do not boast of wealth and act arrogantly.

2. The highly educated must not underestimate others.

3. Speak in a low voice with respect to seniors and elders.

4. Be polite and chivalrous in front of ladies.

Bridging, Range, Distance, Cont'd: 18 Buddha Hands, offensive or defensive, may be used as a bridge and their turning power then used for immediate striking. If there exists a bridge then cross the bridge. If no bridge exists then make a bridge. If under the bridge then return to the top. If on top of the bridge then stay on top and immediately cross to the opponent, Cont'd

Eighteen Buddha Hands

5. No one-sided talk on behalf of money.
6. Do not blame yourself in poor living.
7. Speak the necessary words and keep from excess with silence.
8. Patience is the antidote for curing anger.
9. Do not exaggerate or speak untrue.
10. Do not boast of yourself.
11. Do not criticize others.
12. Do not indulge yourself in imagination.
13. Do not be stubborn to your point of view.
14. Always be wholesome.

These guidelines come from the function of the body and are considered **Ming Kung**.

Visualize a stream of yellow light passing through and washing every cell of your heart. All toxic accumulations are removed as each cell receives currents of healing light from the very throne of God. This is **Hsing Kung**.

Ming Kung and Hsing Kung cannot be separated. Their union leads to development in Chi Kung (qigong). Review the pages above concerning cultivation of the Original Nature and the importance of Right Action. Your Kungfu training, internal or external, will be of no use, only one-sided, without this understanding.

Hsing Ming Kung must be your daily attitude.

Bridging, Range, Distance, Cont'd: Regular training may make one aggressive in nature without the attitude of Hsing Ming Kung. And the constant rubbing, feeling, and turning of power gives one confidence to defeat the enemy.

About the Kungfu: Principles

Song of the Mantis Body Posture

The beginning and the end of training starts with the proper mantis body posture and stance. The song of body posture is a mnemonic device:

Legs are bent like a frog;
Heel-to-toe, shoulder width apart
Hands held like a beggar (asking)
Feet look like "ding" but not ding
Feet look like "ba" but not ba
Raise the perineum
Pull up the stomach
Open and close the rib cage
Round the shoulders
Sink the chest and raise the back
Hand to hand; Heart to heart
You don't come
I won't start
You start first
I hit first

Master Gin Foon Mark, early days

Posture practice according to the above instruction will insure correct alignment of the anterior and posterior (chi) energy chan-

Hakka Mantis Body Posture: Eyes to eyes, hand to hand, heart to heart—you don't come—I won't start. You start and I will hit you first and continuously until you see red (blood). Hands extended like a beggar, legs bent like a frog. Heel-to-toe, centered and shoulder width apart. Pull up the stomach, push down the ribs, elbows sink to the front.

Eighteen Buddha Hands

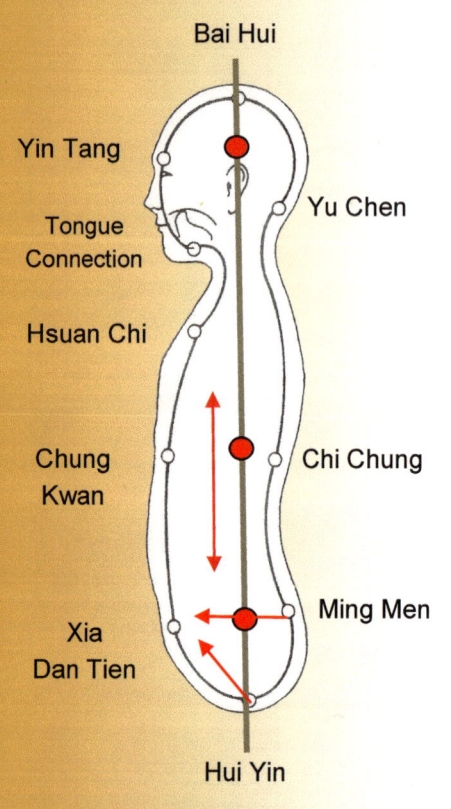

Bai Hui
Yin Tang
Tongue Connection
Hsuan Chi
Yu Chen
Chung Kwan
Chi Chung
Ming Men
Xia Dan Tien
Hui Yin

Tuck the pelvis, raise the perineum, relax the diaphragm, open and close the rib cage in breathing

nels which allows free circulation of blood and facilitates proper relaxed deep breathing.

Imagine a water hose kinked—little water can pass through. Open the kink (straighten the spine) and water flows freely.

When the genuine circulation of heat (energy) pushes through the spine one is said to have developed the root of kungfu.

This is accomplished by tucking the pelvis forward to straighten the curve of the spine allowing the upper, middle and lower "dan tien" centers to be on a straight line through the body.

Of course, this type of "through the back" posture also allows for extension of the arms reach and detraction of the center the center line away from the opponent's attack.

Posture Emulates Mantis: Practitioners emulate the mantis fighting posture by extending their hands forward, with the elbows slightly bent and tucked in close to protect the centerline—like a mantis. The feet are separated slightly wider than your shoulders' width with the lead leg supporting most of the weight, while the slightly curved rear leg acts as a strut.

About the Kungfu: Principles

Weight is 70/30 front to rear. "Heel-to-toe" is the secret of developing the center of gravity and deep rooted posture. Posture, stance and stepping are the foundation and source of power. Horse is father—Mor Sao grinding hand, is mother of mantis.

Stance looks like the Chinese character **"ding"**

丁

But it is not "ding"

Stance looks like the Chinese character **"ba" or eight**

八

But it is not "ba"

This means the stance is not a T stance as in Karate or TKD. And not a double weighted riding horse as in southern styles. But is something of both, but neither one.

Contract and expand the ribcage

Late Sibok Harry Sun

Legs are bent, Feet are heel-to-toe on line, Feet are like "T" and 8" but not, round the back, extend the hands

Rib Cage Power: Opening and closing the rib cage is like an accordion opening and closing. It adds sink and float power as well as closes the distance between the rib bones, making it more difficult to attack the inner organs which they protect. The chambered hands above the heart also are secondary protection of the inner organs—like an exoskeleton.

Eighteen Buddha Hands

Song of the Mantis Body Posture

The "hand to hand" chamber position serves three purposes.

Many will find that the required twisting and turning of the arms greatly increases flexibility of the muscles and tendons and adds to explosive spring power release.

Two, like the insect's exoskeleton, the forearms and hands are an outer cover to protect the torso and inner organs.

And third, perhaps by coincidence, during the late Ching dynasty, placing the back of the hands together was a symbol that signified one had "turned their back" on the Manchurian oppressors and was often seen when the slogan, "fang ching fuk ming" (overthrow the Ching-restore the Ming) was heard. Having shown the "hand to hand signal" one could be recognized as a member of the same group.

"Heart to Heart" teaches that one should focus on defense and protecting the centerline in combat. As one teacher stated, "there is no first strike in traditional martial art." Mantis is defense first.

Unlike many styles who prefer to turn the body sideways to the

Hands Chambered on Chest: This Mantis chambered hands position adds twisting spring power, protects the centerline and internal organs by covering with the forearms and hands, and is symbolic of a "standard" in Southern Praying Mantis.

About the Kungfu: Principles

opponent to lessen their target area, Southern Mantis prefers to remain square to the opponent drawing him into the centerline where numerous mantis traps and pass offs are employed with the forward extended hands.

Esoterically, the saying "heart to heart" symbolizes one's inclusion in the "brotherhood of man" and the practice of "centering" physically, mentally and spiritually. "Heart to heart, you don't come, I won't start" signifies that one has cultivated a spirit of compassion and not aggression.

It is against the law of nature for one to attack another human being, and the person who attacks another, in his heart, will know he is wrong. And what starts wrong cannot end up right. To attack another in aggression is against natural law and eventually one will reap what he has sown. Therefore the saying, "heart to heart" teaches one to be in accord with nature.

"You start first, I hit first" teaches the principle of "giving up oneself to follow others." That is, mantis is a self defense art. One centers, waiting in a static posture, to overcome those in motion. If the opponent wants to hit, he must come close enough so that his arms or legs will reach. When he closes, relax, sink and use listening energy and feeling hand. Then if he is fast or slow, you are fast or slow. At his slightest movement you be able to strike first.

Rooting and centering follows.

Mantis Summarized in Three: Relax, sink and root, use feeling hand and turning power to strike the vital points—this Is the summation of mantis boxing. That is to say mantis is based on a deep rooted horse, borrowing the opponent's force, and attacking his weak and vital points. (Root, Feeling Hand, Vital Points)

Rooting and Centering

Martial Intent is first discussed in boxing principles. Some trainees are warriors by nature and some develop will power and intent through training. Without this primary principle there will be no focus of the body and mind into one purpose.

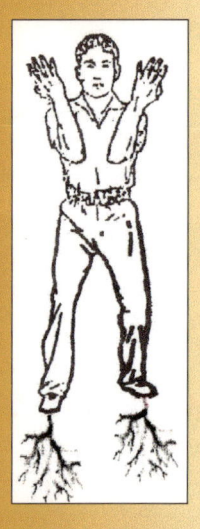

Rooting is next discussed. Rooting is the skill of developing the force of one thousand pounds in the feet. With it the stance is as firm as Mt. Dragon Tiger and not easily moved. Without rooting, the power of the fist will be stagnated in the chest and one's feet will not be steady allowing him to be easily thrown about.

Centering is the development of the root. It is the lowering of the center of gravity within the body. It is accomplished by relaxation, breathing and correct body structure.

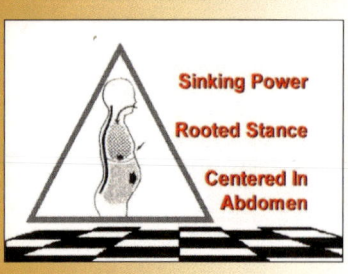

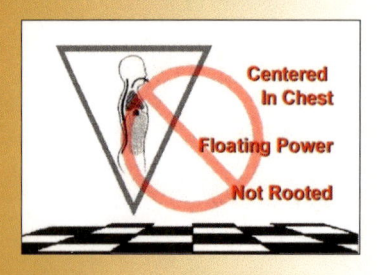

Body structure is a key element. Like a triangle, one must develop a base in relationship with the other parts.

Centering is a sinking power. If the stance is too wide, too narrow, too long or too short, the center will be unstable.

Imagine an upside down triangle standing on it's tip and you can see the slightest force will cause it to topple. This is a floating center and should be avoided.

About the Kungfu: Principles

Many styles mimic the movements of animals, but Jook Lum Temple Mantis is based on the structure of the human being. The practitioner stands upright with the feet firmly placed heel-to-toe and slightly wider than shoulder width. Gathered through the feet and up the legs and back, the power is expressed in the hands. This produces a live springy power (action-reaction force in a sticky way). It is produced by the whole body in spiraling motions, as a spring is twisted and then released. It is the function of the hand and foot arriving at the target intently at the same time. There is a saying, "any deficiency of power in the hand can be found in the footwork (root and center)."

Being that the structure of this kungfu is based on the natural movements of man and the hand movements of a mantis, the style's form and function express themselves as one. How many times have we seen dozens of different stylists, all practicing their various forms, only to enter the fighting competition and become indistinguishable from each other? That is to say, that their form and function are not the same. Jook Lum Mantis is one style that exhibits form and function inseparably.

One must learn to move his center while remaining stable in all positions. This is the function of stepping and is based on the body posture and the use of power in attack and defense with the feet, shins, knees and hips. Jook Lum Temple boxing has both linear and circular stepping such as three steps forward, four corners and eight directions.

Once a rooted stance is developed and one is able to move the

Deep Root—Iron Steps: Strong legs and loose shoulders and the chi energy will sink down. The root will be deep and the iron steps firm and steady. If one cannot root, stick with the opponent and neutralize his force, after years of training he will always be controlled by his opponent.

center of his body by stepping forcefully and aggressively without a break in the root, he may learn to "box" using the hand. When the stance is rooted and one can move the center, it is said the whole body has become a hand.

When walking the (horse) steps, one must step and stop to self-adjust all aspects of the stance and posture before walking another step. After "one thousand perfect steps" one may begin to root unconsciously. Crawl before walking, walk before running.

The mantis arm is composed of three "hands;" from the shoulder to the elbow, from the elbow to the wrist and from the wrist to the fingertips. A good mantis will use his "second hand" for control by pressing the forearm into the centerline of his prey, at the same time striking a vital area with his "first" hand or fingers. Thus, there is constant pressure on the opponent's root and centerline and then a redirection and use of the opponent's resisting force turned against him.

The centered and rooted posture must be expressed in a slight forward momentum to create a forward driving force in attack. One cannot maintain a chest upright posture, or a slight leaning back posture and produce forward driving force. So a driving forward momentum, without over extending, is trained to produce full force. It is said the forward bent knee cannot extend beyond the toes. One must see the tip of the toes when looking down over the knee.

Sever the Root: Sever the opponent's root and center of gravity so that he can be defeated quickly and certainly. One must develop the ability to disrupt the balance of an opponent by "feeling" where his center of gravity is and exploiting it by severing the root.

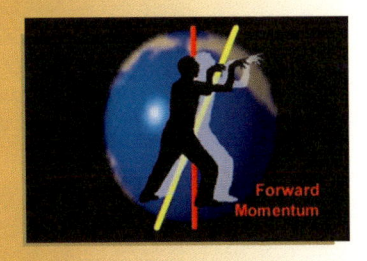

About the Kungfu: Principles

This forward momentum mimics the axis of the earth which is not upright but inclined forward.

One must develop this forward momentum in stance and walking the horse to produce a forward driving power. One cannot stand "chest upright" or sit back on the rear leg. To drive forward one must develop "forward momentum."

Forward momentum in posture and footwork is also a type of "spiral power" likened to the earth spiraling around the sun and turning on its axis at the same time.

Spiral Power in Hakka Mantis

Spiral power in Mantis is produced by the whole body "as a spring is twisted and then released." It is two-fold; a straight forward strike and a simultaneous rotation. It is unity of the straight line and curve in one motion—a spiral line. Like a bullet which moves forward and spirals; like the earth which turns both around the sun and on its axis.

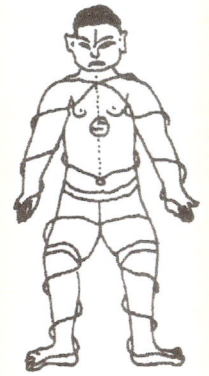

This is accomplished as the hand moves, the arm rotates, the weight transfers from leg to leg and matching spiral movements are made

---

Forward Momentum: The centered and rooted posture must be expressed in a slight forward momentum to create a forward driving force in attack. This forward momentum mimics the axis of the earth which is not upright but inclined. Energy is drawn from the earth through the soles of the feet, up the legs, through the back and out to the fingertips.

44

Eighteen Buddha Hands

by the heel, ankle and knee. This can be seen in correct Taijiquan practice. In short, the whole body spirals power from the ground up.

This is further likened to a car moving forward at 60 mph that strikes a solid wall. The impact will be considerable. But the impact of the same car moving forward at 60 mph while spiraling clockwise at 60 mph will be much greater.

Such spiral power may be clockwise (offensive) or counter clockwise (defensive).

Offensive clockwise spiral power starts at the navel and spirals clockwise over the shoulder, winds around the elbow, and is transferred to the fingers with the palm turned out. This is attacking spiral power.

Defensive spiral power starts counterclockwise from the fingers, winds around the arm, passes the elbow, ascends to the elbow and returns to the navel.

Spiraling power in the legs starts at the navel, circles inside the thighs, circles the knee, calf, ankle, heel, center of the foot and ends at the big toe clockwise. Counter clockwise spiral power starts at the big toe and circles back to the navel.

Spiral power can hardly be understood until one has fully understood the basic method of practicing.

Spiral Power: In attack, spit out the spiraling spring power from the navel to the hands and fingertips. In defense, swallow using spiral power from the fingertips to the navel. This power is mimicked in the legs and feet.

About the Kungfu: Principles

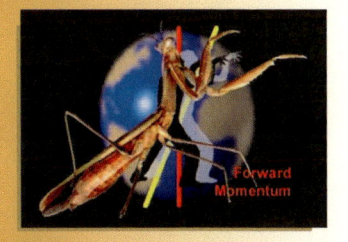

Simply stated, spiral power is illustrated by the karate chop which has the added power of a wrist and elbow twist or snap at the end.

Spiral power is a "ging" explosive force which is rooted in the feet and burst out in the legs, is controlled by the waist and functions through the fingers. From the feet to the legs, legs to the waist, waist to the fingers, the whole body is moved as one unit.

In Southern Praying Mantis, spiral power is expressed in swallow and spit.

Centerline Theory in Hakka Mantis

Centerline theory is similar to pistol training. To stop a man dead in his tracks, destroy the brain; secondary target, the heart, although the aggressor may continue to live and fight several minutes.

The next weakest links in the chain of life are the internal organs. All these lie on the center line. In mantis the forearms and elbows are used to protect the centerline.

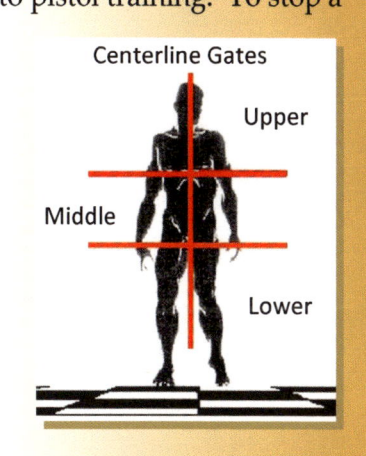

Iron Steps: Iron steps are firm but flexible, hear the opponent's sound, see his shadow, move accordingly. Issue ging explosive power from the wrists, elbows, shoulders, hips, knees, and ankles. Inside, outside, up, down, forward and back. The whole body is one unit.

46

Eighteen Buddha Hands

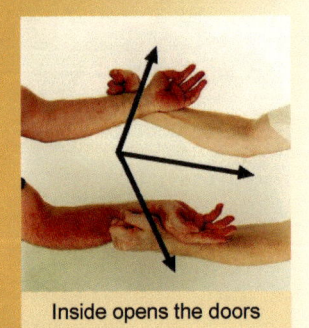

Inside opens the doors

When defending the centerline one must use the mantis inside and outside hooking skills to control the opponent with a slicing

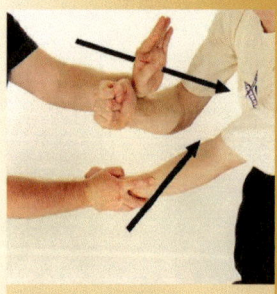

Outside closes the doors

and redirecting hand rather than banging force against force.

Each of the 18 basic hand skills must also be trained three ways; defense only, defense and strike with the same hand, defense and strike with the opposite hand.

Centerline also teaches the 12-6; 3-9 strategy. The maxim is, "make a noise in the north, attack in south. Create a fire in the west, attack in the east."

This teaches "feinting" — a mock attack aimed at one place or point merely as a distraction from the real place or point of attack.

This is taught in the 108 form.

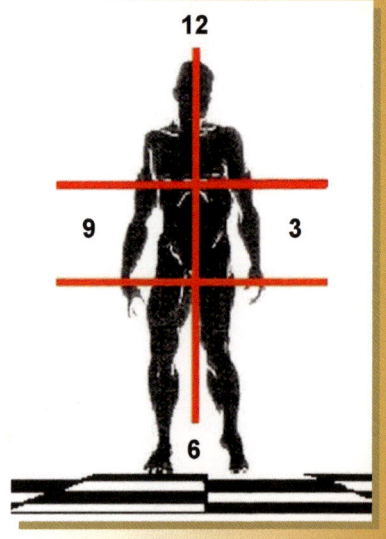

Deficiency of Power: A maxim states, "any deficiency of power in the hand, can be found in the root and center. The rooted horse is the father, Mor Sao feeling hand is the mother." When rooting, spring and spiral power becomes skillful, one feels as if he is anchored or rooted fully to the earth.

About the Kungfu: Principles

Contact, Control, Strike Continuously

Contact by making or crossing the bridge, control by neutralizing or borrowing the opponent's force and strike continuously until red flows (the opponent bleeds). This is central to all Hakka Mantis.

One Arm—Three Hands

The Mantis arm is composed of three "hands"—from the shoulder to the elbow, from the elbow to the wrist and the wrist to the fingertips. A good Mantis will use the "second hand" for control by pressing his forearm into the centerline of his prey, at the same time striking a vital area with his "first" hand or fingers.

This simultaneous defend and attack with one arm is done by using the forearm for defensive movement while attacking the hand or fingers. This can only be understood if one has understood the centerline theory.

A skillful Mantis will defend and attack using one arm to trap and control the opponent's two arms, leaving one hand free to attack at will. (photo above - late Sibok Harry Sun)

Contact, Control, Strike: The principle of contact, control, and strike (until the opponent is red) is central to all Hakka Mantis action and is based on the three powers of the arm; from the shoulder to the elbow, elbow to the wrist, wrist to the fingertips.

Eighteen Buddha Hands

Intercepting and Sticky Hand

Engage the opponent by intercepting his attack and then remaining sticky—feeling his intent. Intercepting is broken power likened to western boxing. One attacks—withdraws, attacks—withdraws in broken contact. However, once contact is made, sticky hand attaches to the opponent like glue and the opponent cannot separate.

Sticky training is to learn relaxation. It is the ability to not blink when being struck. It is the attaching to the center of the opponent's being, neither pushing into nor pulling away from him. It is being perfectly attached in stillness and motion.

Feeling hand is the result of sticky hand. One must learn to neither anticipate the opponent's movement nor telegraph his own.

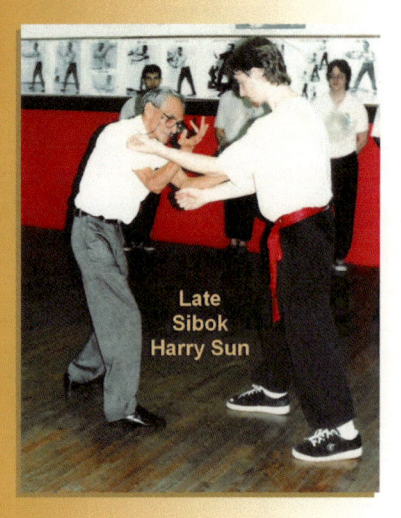

Late Sibok Harry Sun

Feeling hand is the reading of the opponent's intent. It is as if the hand (whole body is a hand) has an eye of it's own. With feeling hand one learns to control the opponent by jamming, trapping, deflecting and attacking the opponent's intent. This done based on the control points of the body.

Control the elbows and you will control his arms. Control his knee and you will control his leg.

Knowing Self and Others: Sticky hand and two man training is to know others. Single man forms and shadowboxing is to know one's self. Attach and stick to the opponent neither pushing into nor pulling away—the hand simply sticks and listens to the opponent's intent.

Single—Double Bridge; Anticipating—Telegraphing

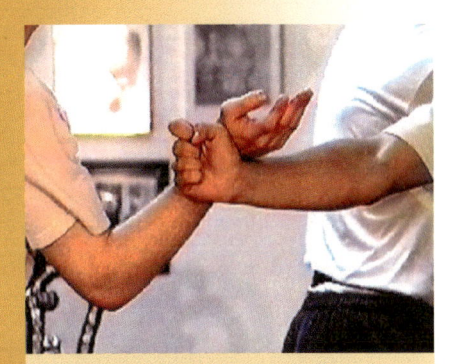

Single Bridge—Outside

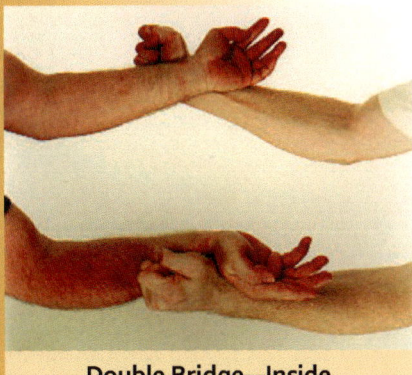

Double Bridge—Inside

Defense and attack may be with one hand or two; single or double bridge, inside or outside. Triple bridging is the use of two arms and one leg or foot.

Although all eighteen basic hand skills may be employed in either single or double bridge, Sai Shu and Han Shu are less common in double bridge variation.

As well, all eighteen hands may be employed inside or outside the opponent's gate. Between the opponent's arms is inside his gate. It is advantageous to bridge from the outside.

Anticipating is moving or reacting to what one believes the opponent is going to do before he moves. Telegraphing is fidgeting or displaying your intention before you act. One must avoid both anticipating and telegraphing. Instead, root and use feeling hand to turn his power against him.

Hand and Foot Together—Whole Body As One: The hand moves, the arm rotates and the weight is transferred from the ground up the heels, ankles, knees, and hips. The hand and foot arrives at the target intently at the same time.

Dead and Live Power

If one's power, cannot be easily changed according to the opponent's reaction, power, and intent then it is called "dead power". We see this in many Karate movements where force is met with greater force. It is "dead" because once exerted it usually cannot change or re-issue power until it has been generated by chambering or pulling back the hand as in the reverse punch. It is dead because it cannot feel, stick, and turn according to the opponent's movement and intent.

In contrast, "live power" strikes, sticks to, follows and regenerates power by using the opponent's movement. The power is continuous and flowing without the need for pulling back the hand or recoiling the arm. One blow changes to another blow without ever breaking contact and always following the opponent's force. This is refined in the two man training and two man forms.

Lik and Ging Power—Natural and Refined Strength

Lik (li) is the natural strength a man's body possesses. It is his physical constitution and it varies from person to person. Sometimes a smaller person is naturally stronger than a larger person and sometimes the larger person is not naturally strong. In the case of one's Lik (natural strength) size is not always an indicator.

Ging (jing) is based on the Lik (natural strength) of a person, but it is not natural. It is a refined strength, a strength that is acquired after special training.

Dead and Live: One must train two man feeling hands in a live way to understand the principle of contact, control and strike until red. It is of a sticky nature. Otherwise, banging of arms is simply dead power, force against force, without turning or borrowing power.

About the Kungfu: Principles

Think of the body builder. He has both lik and ging. His natural strength (lik) is due to his body size and his refined strength (ging) is developed in the movement of lifting weights. Therefore, his ging is useful in moving weights, but not necessarily in boxing. This is why different people with different daily lives have different lik and ging. The person who digs ditches with a shovel will develop a refined power (ging) that allows him the greatest ease and comfort at shoveling. And so it is that in martial art we develop ging or refined power after special training. And we can see that the better our (lik) natural strength the greater our refined strength will also be. Today, we can hear of so many kinds of ging, particularly in Tai Chi or the so named "internal arts", that it may sound confusing. Simply stated, each skill or technique, when mastered, becomes a ging.

Martial artists speak of "fa jing or fat ging", that is the issuing, emitting or sending forth of refined strength by various skills. In mantis, the term, ging, is used as an overall word indicating refined strength and each technique or special skill is simply called a "hand". However, each of the 18 mantis basic hands could be called a ging, (Mor ging, Gwak ging, Choc ging, etc.) because after repeated training one will acquire extraordinary power in this particular motion. Use your (lik) natural strength to refine your kungfu explosive power (ging).

It is said that ging is produced in the feet and expressed outward toward the limbs. This is the function of the stance and footwork. If not exactly correct, one may never develop a root and center and so the hands will never develop sufficient ging. Pay special attention to heel-to-toe and the internal work.

Natural and Refined: Neither natural nor refined strength will ensure victory over the opponent. But, by daily training your refined strength in the various boxing skills will increase the likelihood of a successful outcome in a fight. When two tigers of equal power and skill engage, fate determines the outcome.

Eighteen Buddha Hands

Form and Function

In most teachings, forms are broken down into a sequence of 1, 2, or 3 techniques (movements) and explained as combat application. The problem with this is that the demonstration is usually static; this is, one person is asked to punch (attack) and hold out his hand while the other applies a sequence of 1-2-3 actions in defense and offense. This is unrealistic. In a real fight the attacker will never punch only once and stop - waiting for your reaction. Neither will he remain static waiting for you to attack him (or his weak spots). Action causes reaction - this is a basic law of nature (and survival).

Late Sibok Harry Sun

When one person defends and/or attacks the other will instinctually move to avoid being hit - in example, clap your hands in a wilderness area and watch as the fowl and animals instinctually move - or like one automatically blinks when being poked toward the eyes.

Martial arts applications cannot be realistic if they are static. Application must be dynamic; cause and effect, action and reaction, especially against skilled martial artists. It is possible that a skilled martial artist defending against an unskilled person MIGHT find himself in a situation where his 1, 2, 3 movement can be applied,

Ging Not Buffalo Strength: Crossing hands one attempts to diffuse incoming forces by feeling and redirecting them. One should use refined force and technique and not reply on buffalo strength or brute force.

About the Kungfu: Principles

but, even an unskilled person will turn his head when being struck in the face or turn his body when being struck in the chest.

Therefore, superior martial art must first be guided by relentless intent - eye to eye, hand to hand, driving forward into the center of the opponent's being. Second, a superior skill must have segmented feeling power which can produce whole body force. That is, any part of the body can yield independently to the opponent's incoming force creating an unstable center and opening and then discharge a focused single deadly strike with power issuing from the feet, up the legs, back, arms, and fingers into a weak vital point of the opponent such as the eyes, throat, or solar plexus. Third, a skillful art must be based on changes of the hand, since the hand (arm) is the quickest and most convenient weapon (just watch any real fight).

By pressing the centerline of the opponent, sticking to his movement and feeling his intent, the skillful hand can, using small, quick, short, angular jerks and deflections, redirect and create an opening in the opponent's center and intent while delivering a single devastating blow in a straight line (the shortest quickest distance between two points) to his vital spots. Continuous direct blows are given until the opponent's submission. The mantis philosophy is train until within three blows the opponent submits, bleeds or ceases to exist.

But this is based on the ability of the practitioner to intently stick, feel, yield and discharge continuous changes based on the opponent's action and reaction. Simply said, if pushed downward the hand turns to strike upward, if pushed upward the hand turns to

One Ging Expressed in Different Hands: There is only one "ging" (refined natural body power) but expressed differently in the 18 Hands (Mor Ging, Gwak Ging, Choc Ging) and various boxing skills. From the feet, waist, and shoulders power will arrive in the hands.

Form and Function

strike downward, if pushed inward the hand turns to strike outward, if pushed out the hand turns (changes) to strike inward. Of course, this is a principle and as one becomes skillful, his hand learns to adapt to any angle or circumstance. Like the stance, one first finds the center, develops power, moves the center and attaches the center to his opponent. Later, any position or posture is centered, whether lying, sitting, standing or walking.

The eighteen mantis hands all change in this way without a break in the power and contact of the two people. A is followed by B, by C turns to D and so on. In time, two people learn to change hands (power) automatically. By repetition, A instinctu-

Frightening Spring Power : Ging is likened to a "frightened reaction" - it is an automatic instinctual response. When one touches a burning stove the hand immediately and quickly jerks away. When sensitivity is refined the 18 hands will react the same way when crossing hands with others.

About the Kungfu: Principles

ally turns to B turns to C, etc. At this point, one may simply hold out his hands and they will move and strike without thought. When the eighteen mantis hands are practiced by two skillful people, it looks like a continuous "sticky" fight. Once contact is made there is no backing up or breaking apart. Each of the eighteen hands is a reaction to an action with the intent of each movement to make one deadly strike enough. Learning the eighteen hand changes individually is basic training and is followed by a series of two man "sticky, feeling, changing power" forms in which the mantis practitioners begin to instinctually skill various changes while developing precision in striking vital areas. The forms are "hands on" and realistic in "continuous fighting" teaching action—reaction.

And so, a superior art is based on a deep rooted stance, upright footwork in stepping and production of power by the movement of the ribs and diaphragm. It will use the conditioned arms and hands 70% of the time and the legs and feet 30% of the time in offense and defense. Again, this is because the hands are the quickest and most convenient weapon (as seen in a real fight).

3 Methods of Bridging; Crushing, Swallowing, Evading

A bridge is any part of the body used to close the distance to the opponent. Arm and hands are commonly the bridge.

Three methods are hard bridge (smash thru the opponent); soft bridge (borrowing force); and evasive bridge (contact with the opponent is avoided or neutralized). Any and each of the 18 offensive and defensive hands may be used as a

Superior Art: A superior martial art will use the conditioned arms and hands 70% of the time and the legs and feet 30% in offense and defense. This is because the hands are the quickest and most convenient weapon (as seen in a real fight). However, hands and feet should be equally skillful.

bridge and their turning power then used for immediate and continuous striking. If there exists a bridge then cross the bridge. If no bridge exists then make a bridge. If under the bridge then return to the top. If on top of the bridge stay on top and immediately cross.

4 Word Secret; Float, Sink, Swallow, Spit

Four words can summarize the mechanics of Southern Praying Mantis. **Float** is the sudden release of force, explosive energy, which is capable of bouncing the opponent away in full weight. Skillfully applied the opponent will feel like being afloat on water and is easily thrown aside. This energy bounds out in waves. It is similar to "peng" or ward off in Tai chi or I Chuan (Dachengquan).

In mantis this is supplemented by the heavy iron bar rolled over the forearms - pop it up, catch, roll it to the fingertips or by multiple heavy iron rings on the arms. Two man training is primary.

This is expressed as Fic/Ping Shu in the 18 Hands training. The arms flick upward or outward like the insect. Strength comes from the ground through the feet and spine.

Sink is more difficult to master because it depends on one's natural ability to learn "feeling" or perceive the opponent's exertion of force. He who has mastered this is capable of rendering his opponent completely immobile, thus putting him under absolute control. When the opponent moves, one simply sinks the center into him. This is trained in the "three" form—sombogin.

Swallow and Spit: In essence, the nine defensive hands are "swallow" and the nine offensive hands are "spit". Memorize the meaning and visualize this in your training of the 18 Hands.

About the Kungfu: Principles

Energy is expressed from the lower "Dan Tien" behind the navel.

Swallow is the exertion of flexible force usually in circular manners, and linear, so that you intercept the opponent's blow by causing it slide and miss the target, rather than intercepting it by force against force. This is practiced in all mantis hands.

Spit means to strike; to strike using the borrowed force of the opponent; to strike in such a way that the opponent feels swallow and spit, sink, float, in one strike.

If skillfully applied some say this feels like the opponent is being shocked by electricity.

These four characters sum up the secret of Southern Praying Mantis techniques.

One Four Word Secret of Ging
Float—Ping Shu
Sink—Bao Zhang
Swallow—Gop Shu
Spit—Jek Shu

Internal Training

Southern Mantis is an internal art. Power is generated from the feet up the legs thru the back and out to the hands. Internal power cannot be generated unless shoulders are relaxed and the elbows dropped, pointing down.

In many styles, during the standard reverse punch the elbows

Float and Sink: Float and sink are functions of posture and ging and are the structural power for swallow and spit.

Internal Training

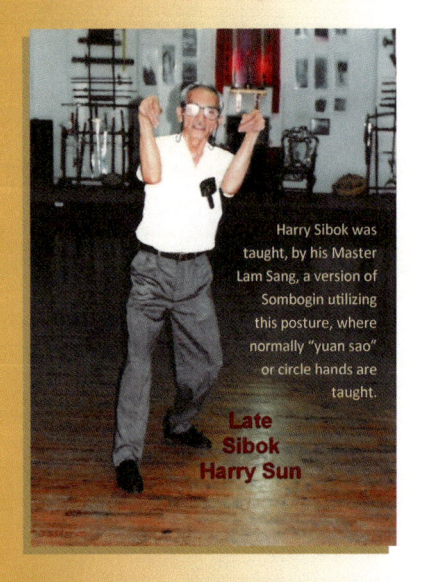

Harry Sibok was taught, by his Master Lam Sang, a version of Sombogin utilizing this posture, where normally "yuan sao" or circle hands are taught.

Late Sibok Harry Sun

turn outside instead of down toward earth.

Elbows down is critical to issuing whole body power. It is said that when the elbows are down one issues the dynamic power of tendons and sinews. When the elbows are pointed to the outside one issues the static power of the skeleton and muscles.

With age the skeleton becomes brittle and the muscles atrophy even to those who practice daily in advanced years. Yet the dynamic power of tendons and sinews will increase as one practices in advanced age. Therefore it;s important to first train the structural internal power, then the physical external power. Even with daily training, one's physical power will decrease with age, but one's internal structural power will increase with age.

Internal training can lead to success in old age but the wrong structural power will lead to failure. Age deteriorates the muscles and skeleton. Internal training is twofold: structural power and internal organ control.

Structural power is critical to martial art and self defense. One may have internal organ and breath control but not be able to use it for martial purposes.

Internal Training is Structure and Organ Control: It is important to first train the structural internal power and then the physical external power. Even with daily training, one's physical power will decrease with age, but one's internal structural power will increase with age.

About the Kungfu: Principles

Structural power is developing the center of gravity. It is centering and rooting until the stance is as solid and firm as Mt. Tai. Someone rooted this way feels bolted to the floor. It is said that once a practitioner centers he may move and attach to his opponent's center rendering him unable to move. One's self defense ability increases in relation to the establishment of his center. Of course, centering extends to mind and spirit once the body is trained.

To establish a physical centering, one may observe the following 18 points:

1. Relax. Stand flat-footed. In mantis, this must include feet heel-to-toe slightly wider than shoulders. Grip with the toes.
2. Bend the knees slightly.
3. Relax the hips.
4. Round the crotch or tuck the pelvis.
5. Lift the anus.
6. Pull up the stomach.
7. Relax the waist.
8. Close the ribs.
9. Tuck in or concave the chest.
10. Stretch and round the back.
11. Drop the shoulders.
12. Drop the elbows.

18 Points of Postural Adjustment: Holding your standing horse for 18 minutes while adjusting the 18 points listed above will correctly align and allow the breath to circulate up the anterior and down the posterior channels. This is the foundation of rooting.

Internal Training

13. Hollow the armpits.
14. Relax the wrists.
15. Suspend the head; tuck the chin.
16. Close the mouth. Clinch the molars slightly.
17. Tongue up.
18. Eyes bright.

This internal structure will lead to a centered dynamic fluid lively flexible power - an internal power.

This internal structural power must be augmented with internal breath and organ control. The ability to open and close the body by way of the force of breath combined with inner contraction and expansion of the organs and rib cage completes ones internal force.

Circulation of the Breath

Internal strength is postural adjustment and correct breathing. A proverb states, the beginning of kungfu training is completion of the minor circulation of breath (chi) around the torso (hsiao chou tien). It is said centering and rooting begins with the small breath circulation.

So one may develop internal power by adjusting his stance or structure and controlling the inner function of breath and organ control.

Minor Circulation is the Foundation: Postural adjustment and correct breath control create internal strength. Rooting and centering the horse stance begins with this internal work.

About the Kungfu: Principles

Yet, internal power may be trained but not useful for self defense. Various internal methods all must follow the same principles only some with emphasis on meditation and health and some with emphasis on martial art and self defense.

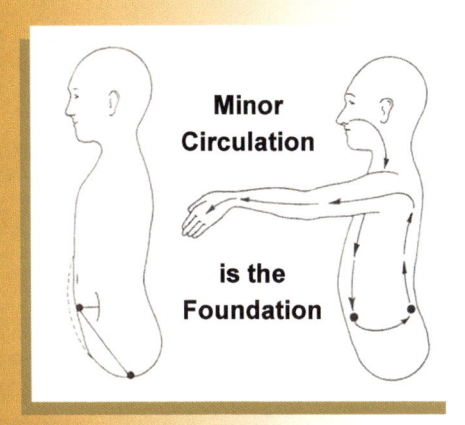

Minor Circulation is the Foundation

Health is a by-product of martial art training but internal training alone will not produce self defense ability.

Southern Praying Mantis is based on using this internal power for self defense and good health is a secondary result.

There is no secret mysterious internal power. There is only the structural and internal control that may produce a mysterious result.

Da Mak—Dim Mak Vital Point Striking

One of the unique features of Southern Praying Mantis emphasizes is "da-mak" and "dim-mak" in striking. This may be loosely compared to a "thrust" and a "snap" punch.

Mak is a point. Da or Dim is a method of striking. Although every style has some form of "da-mak", a straight punch or strike, dim is somewhat unique in that is more than a snap, it's a spring power using the whole body as a whip with the energy explod-

Correct Breathing is Essential: Train deep breathing with the diaphragm — inhale expand the abdomen, exhale—contract the abdomen. Do not breathe shallow with the chest. Inhale and swallow, exhale and spit. One may hold the breath when striking.

Da Mak—Dim Mak Vital Point Striking

ing from the phoenix eye fist or fingertip. It uses the flexible force of the elbow and wrist joints to add to the spring power.

"Dim" is a precise finger or knuckle attack with spring power to a precise point or "mak".

Vital Point Striking

Instant Death, stopping the enemy in his tracks—these are the goals of vital point striking. Although, the notion of striking (or lightly touching) someone and them dying days, weeks or months later has appeal, it will not be preferable in the reality of facing an opponent who is larger and stronger or when facing multiple enemy in hand to hand combat. Fact being, it will be necessary to maim or kill the enemy as quickly as possible to avoid danger to yourself.

There are only three ways to accomplish this: destroy the circulatory system and stop the flow of blood; destroy the respiratory system and stop the ability to breathe; or destroy the Central Nervous System (brain and spinal cord). Of these three methods, destroying the brain is the quickest and will immediately incapacitate the enemy.

By stopping the blood circulation to the brain (one method is destroying the carotid artery located at a depth of 1.5 inches on the side of the neck) the average enemy will probably go unconscious in less than 60 seconds, thereby giving him a full minute to continue trying to destroy you!

On Guard
Sibok Harry Sun

About the Kungfu: Principles

Stopping the ability to breathe will usually incapacitate the enemy within one minute, although he may live several minutes longer. A skilled (even unskilled) strike to the hyoid bone (top of the throat) or the trachea (bottom of the throat) can destroy the respiratory system and stop the average enemy within 20 seconds, although he may continue to engage you.

Destroying the brain (or spinal cord) is the quickest way to stop the enemy dead in his tracks. Therein is the rationale for the primary pistol targets: brain and spinal cord. By hand this may be accomplished in a variety of ways:

1. An attack to the vital point behind the ear will result in hemorrhage in the brain tissue and between its membranes (dura mater and pia mater);

2. An attack (concussive vibration) to the top (fontanelles) of the skull would cause bleeding in the brain tissue and subarachnoid hemorrhages with possible fractures of the skull bones;

3. An attack to the base of the skull or near the nape of the neck can lead to fracture of the odontoid process of the second (Axis) cervical vertebra or the transverse process of the first (Atlas) cervical vertebra, accompanied by injury to the vertebral artery and hence severe subarachnoidal hemorrhage. This is one of the dim mak strikes which may leave no visible signs of damage after death.

Other fatal consequences of a trained hand may be:

4, An attack to the thyroid cartilage (above the sternum) may fracture the cartilage causing hemorrhage of the carotid artery and the carotid sinus also causing sudden vagal inhibition with consequent cardiac arrest.

5. An attack to the coeliac (solar) plexus, largest of the sympathetic plexuses, may cause sudden heart stoppage (vagal inhibition) and damage to the liver or coeliac artery as it lies about the level of the first lumbar vertebrae.

Da Mak—Dim Mak Vital Point Striking

Although, any present day medical student could illuminate countless others, the above points illustrate the need to understand striking the enemy's vital points.

A large body of knowledge about the precise points of special sensitivity and danger on the surface of the human body, which in the cause of violent assault, may leave no external sign yet lead to trauma, contusion, shock, internal injury or death has evolved in China from as early as the Han Dynasty (202 BC - 220 AD). The Book of Rites (Li Chi) contains early records detailing the examination of corpses which resulted from violent actions.

In 1247 AD, the Book of Washing Away Unjust Imputations (Hsi Yuan Li) lists and diagrams 32 points of particular danger. Often the vital points correspond with "forbidden" acupuncture and moxibustion points which could induce bleeding, fainting, piercing of the large nerve trunks, etc. By 1644 the methods of striking these points and intercepting their meridians were highly developed.

Even an unskilled blow by the average man at the right place and time can be fatal and the Yin and Yang of the body is that it is at once both fragile and extremely resilient. Numerous are the cases of a man, who being struck or shot multiple times continues his assault. On the other hand, there are freak accidents when for no apparent reason the slightest trauma is lethal. However, as evidenced above, the ancient Chinese knew that the aggression of one unarmed man upon another could be productive of the most fatal consequences if one of the two was trained in the martial art of vital point striking.

When considering vital point training one must familiarize himself with the body's makeup, i.e. the muscular, skeletal, circulatory, respiratory, nervous and digestive systems etc. Knowledge of these structures locations, depths etc. are also required as well as the typography of vital energy circulation (acupuncture).

Next one must familiarize himself with the hand techniques used in striking vital points (i.e. striking with the thumbs, fingertips, knuckles, etc, including angle and direction of attack, number of strikes necessary, and so on). Primarily, the hand and fingers will be used although, the feet, elbows, shoulders, and head can be used, with less efficiency. Conditioning of these tools is also necessary for maximum result. With proper training the fingers can truly become like daggers (or needles wrapped in cotton) which will rip or pierce the enemy's flesh from his bones.

Without power and speed it is not possible to effectively strike vital points. One must develop the knocking power of concussive vibrations, the penetrating power to damage structures at a depth of 6 inches internally and the grasping power to damage joints, cartilage, nerves and skin. As many as 3 points may be attacked in one movement. However, without the knowledge and familiarization of the internal structures, one cannot focus his intention or will to destroy them.

Other factors also come to play in vital point striking. Breathing, muscular structure of the enemy, weather and time may influence the result. In reference to time, it has been known in China for 2200 years of the existence of the 24 hour circadian rhythms in the human body (as evidenced in the Huang Ti Nei Ching), although it was not until the 1960s that western science began to study such as routine.

Late Sifu Louie Jack Man

Mor Sao Grinding Hand

Da Mak—Dim Mak Vital Point Striking

These 24 hour rhythms concern hormone secretion and the pineal gland in the head (upper dan tien center) is suspected of being the rhythm regulator. Today, medical science evidences drastic changes in the severity of diseases and symptoms at different times of the day.

However, as for the idea of striking someone and them dying or becoming ill at a later date, I imagine a scenario like this: Ancient China (and perhaps modern rural). Two men fight. One has acute internal damage to his body. Immediate treatment is not available. Life goes on. The man goes back to work. His condition worsens and he dies days, weeks, or several months later from a martial arts blow. Thus, the stuff of Legend and movies is born. And as for the idea of lightly touching someone to induce death or unconsciousness, let us just say the laws of physics don't add up (at any point or structure of the body).

It is ludicrous that today some Karate and Kungfu teachers promote "dim mak" as a light body touch or slap and then by rubbing them on the back bring them back around. Poppycock—dangerous nonsense that it is.

From a military (martial) art standpoint, advanced martial arts training must include the knowledge of the body's weakest points and the knowledge of attacking them to cause the maximum result: death.

108 Vital Points

The metaphors of 108 in Asian culture are too numerous to list here and can be found elsewhere. In mantis, it is the single teaching of vital spots (not necessarily taught in the single or two man set of 108, but has been).

The concept of attacking vital spots is commonplace in Asian folk culture, especially, Chinese. Cheap popular paperbacks and martial art novels common in bookstalls on every corner, espouse the martial master's miraculous powers of supposedly attacking vital spots by simply pointing or looking at them, as well as his psychic ability to control people, tame animals and change the weather.

At the core of such fantastic stories lies a martial practice that has been well documented by various Oriental cultures and their antiquated medical texts. And, although, the principles and practice of striking the vital spots remain constant, the actual location of the spots vary from tradition to tradition.

Chopping, thrusting, slapping, hitting and seizing the flesh, bones, tendons, veins, arteries and joints to defeat an opponent produces an immediate effect - it either stops the opponent or not. The belief that channels of subtle energy circulate through vital spots on the body in a fixed pattern and may be attacked at various times to injure, maim or take life, seems to require a "doubtless mentality"—something akin to the mentality between the faithful and the faith healer.

It is said that this tradition is rarely transmitted to any except those most devout and pure of heart with complete trust in the 'master'. Others say that "knowing the vital spots" is not a knowledge that can be taught, but only "intuited" by those who through long

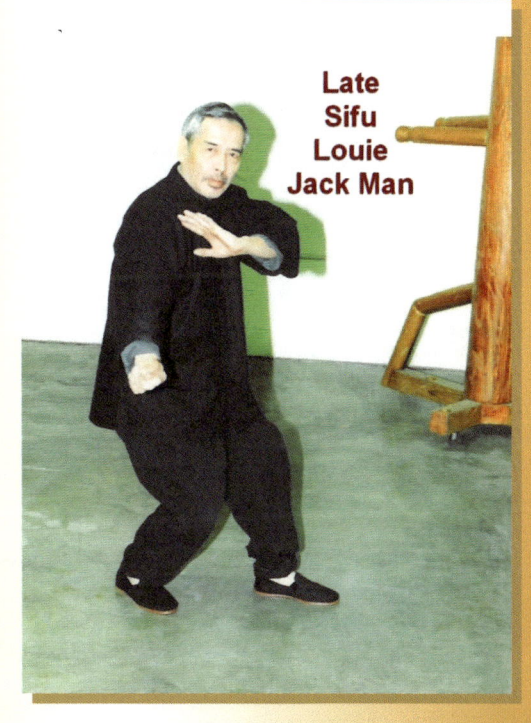

Late Sifu Louie Jack Man

Eighteen Buddha Hands

108 Vital Points

martial training with meditation and spiritual enlightenment can "see" the whole mechanism and inner movements of the body.

The entire body and all its movements become crystal clear. One "intuits" the subtle energy body and its vital points. This "inward eye" experience is said to be wonderful. One needs not grope for a vital center of spot, he can touch it at any given time.

In most Chinese martial traditions, 108 spots are discussed as 36 lethal and 72 paralyzing or less severe, although some traditions indicate 51 spots that lead to immediate death, death with 24 hours, or within one month. Star time, or seasonal rotations and the monthly lunar cycles, are usually an important element in the "108 - four seasons" teaching. Some say the "life force" is located only in one specific vital spot at a time and it moves around the body according to the new and full moon cycles.

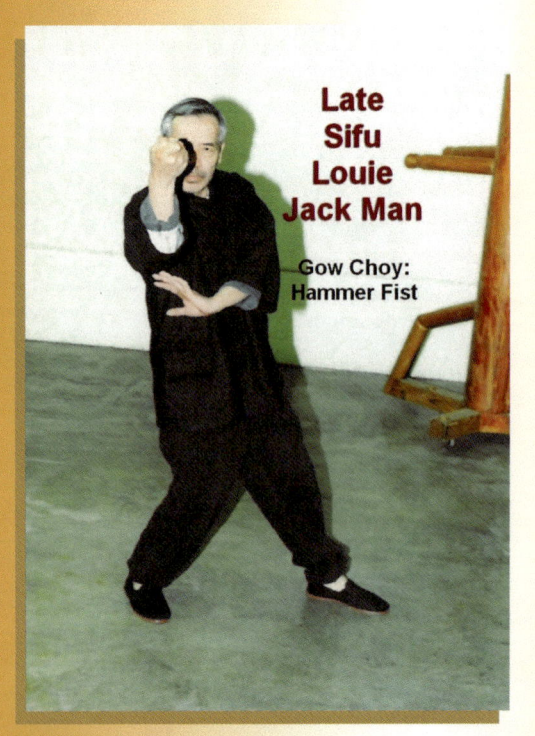

Late Sifu Louie Jack Man

Gow Choy: Hammer Fist

To be successful in attacking the vital spots therefore requires the "inward eye" of self-realization, knowledge of star time and most importantly the practical techniques of fighting applications necessary to locate and attack the particular spots vulnerable. Some also state that one must have first developed the ability to channel his own "vital energy" in order to effectively strike the vital spots.

One tradition enumerates the 108 points as 14 on the arms, 14 on the legs, 9 on the stomach, 46 on the chest and back and 25 on the neck and head. Some points may be symmetrical...double spots. Yet, variations and multiple interpretations in the knowledge and teaching of the vital spots exists today because older martial traditions have (usually or) always been relatively closed and secretive.

Variations in locating the points also exist. Using the distance of one's finger width, each spot may be located and marked with rice paste or some other marker. Or simply by carefully touching / probing the body to feel the precise locations. Some say from the head to the toe about every one inch contains a large spot and every 10th of an inch a small spot. Chinese kungfu usually at it's deepest level, speaks of these 36 large spots and 72 small spots ---108.

It is said that some large spots occur when the vital energy passes closer to the skin surface and are therefore more exposed to stoppage. Small spots occur as the energy goes deeper or circles around the large spots.

Symptoms of injury can be categorized by locations attacked. An example is a point below the chest described as "liquid in nature" and a bit tilted to the right --- when struck properly the result is thick blood flowing, breathing difficulty and consequently worse. Don't search too hard!

When striking vital spots with sharp objects that cause open wounds, the person expires as a result of the vital energy going out through the wound. When a spot is penetrated with a blunt object or blow, the vital energy is stopped at the point of penetration and the entire subtle energy structure may collapse, possibly resulting in death.

When using natural weapons such as various fists, fingers, palms, and elbows, it is said that the opponent's body posture as

108 Vital Points

well as the direction of the attack must be considered. Some spots can only be struck when the opponent's body posture is in the right position and open to that spot. Straight strikes, striking on a forty five degree angle, catching inside and pulling out all depend on the opponent's position. Similarly, breathing patterns or rhythms of respiration may allow access to specific points - striking the opponent between exhalation and inhalation, etc.

Pulling or stretching the opponent while striking in a certain way may allow further access to some points. The second or middle finger is sometimes called the "finger of death" and when the index and middle finger are used together death is avoided as you will only penetrate half way. The five fingers may also be used to attack continuously and one may see what appears to be the master "playing a piano" in a continuous keystroke movement of fingers over the body. But make sure you have "steel fingers" or as sometimes translated "steal fingers". They steal, cheat, and borrow your power.

The philosophy of "Som Dot's" Praying Mantis is that one should never strike first. The practical techniques of attack, defense, and counter application are said to be "pre-measured" in the correct practice of his 108 two man set and/or the direct application of 36/72. That is to say, it is either taught by charts according to seasons with 1, 2, 3 applications and / or the two man 108 set. Imagine a set form that takes two people through 108 points, considering all the above requirements.

Since this type of training is often considered taboo, (like shen gong - spiritual gong - if you use it, karma will come back to you in the form of a great loss), it is no surprise that it requires the opposite skill of healing the injured opponent. You must understand each of the 108 points and their results when attacked, and be able to apply their recovery.

A master's reluctance to impart this type of information is usual-

About the Kungfu: Principles

ly due to either his genuine desire or commitment to follow a tradition of secrecy or to hide the fact that he really doesn't have full knowledge of vital spots. Hence, the kungfu proverb, "those who have attained self-realization" will not exhibit it and those who have not attained are those who exhibit it".

I always thought to follow my Mantis Uncle, Harry Sun, who said, "If you have the power and skill, any spot you hit is a vital spot. A gentleman never hits anyone."

Late Sibok Harry Sun

72

About the Kungfu: Fundamentals

Correct horse stance is the father of power. Mor Sao is the mother of hands. Power is gathered through the feet, up the legs and back, and expressed in the hands. Without a firm stance there is no root and without a root there will be little power in the hands.

Fundamentals in Southern Mantis

Footwork, Forms, Refinements, Supplementals

Boxing principles must be ingrained through fundamental training which includes footwork, two man strengthening and conditioning, hand defense and strikes, elbow strokes, kicks, sweeps, takedowns, qin-na, grappling, single man forms, chi sao, two man forms, apparatus training, breathing exercises, and anatomy — vital point skills.

Traditionally, one may also become acquainted with herbal cures, bone-setting and medicinal practice and even spiritual practices of an esoteric nature.

Eighteen Buddha Hands

Footwork

When one has understood correct posture and internal work (horse stance), he may begin to train "walking the horse" in various footwork patterns which may include "but are not limited to" the following. Note that still photography is not capable of capturing the motion of stepping, therefore, this section does not illustrate all stepping patterns.

Opening the Horse
Technique: Hands chambered over the heart, feet together, raise the left knee—step back, raise the right knee and step forward heel-to-toe, center, sink and root.

Changes: Open on the opposite side; right then left.
Defense: Area from the knee to ankle (shin) defends across the centerline from solar plexus to feet. Foot instep may hook opponent's ankle.
Offense: Knee strikes.

Shuffle Step
Technique: Hands chambered over the heart in a right horse stance. As if standing flush against a wall, shuffle the feet and change the horse right to left and left to right without moving forward or backward. Shuffle semi-circles in place.
Defense: Used when one cannot move forward or backward to adjust the horse and maintain movement.
Offense: Hips, knees, and ankles jam against the opponent's same.

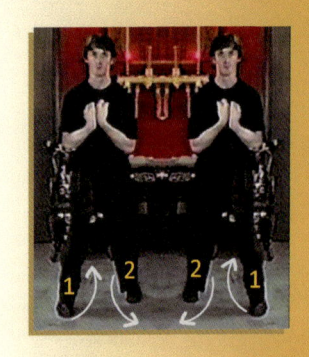

About the Kungfu: Fundamentals

Turnarounds—
Back and Front Foot
Technique: Hands akimbo in a right horse stance. Step across with front foot keeping heel-to-toe on line, place knees to knees with feet shoulder width apart, rise very slightly on the balls of the feet and turn around in the opposite direction. The right horse turns into a left horse behind when the turn is complete.
Changes: Train backfoot turn by stepping across with back foot.
Defense: Evasive step and quickest turn around.
Offense: Step across is a sweep or cross kick at knee level.

Chop Step
Technique:
1) Hands akimbo in a right horse stance. In one motion: 2) Raise the right knee up to solar plexus. 3) Back down ankle to ankle 4) Then step forward six inches while slicing out, skimming the ground toe to heel, bring up the back foot heel-to-toe on line, returning to the right horse. 5) Center, sink, & root.
Changes: Train left, right, then alternating left and right steps in one place; then train 1, 3 and 9 steps forward with turnarounds and return steps.
Attributes: One hard step makes the sound of "bing-bong."
Defense: Area from the knee to ankle (shin) defends across the centerline from solar plexus to feet. Foot instep may hook opponent's ankle.
Offense: Knee strikes (nail knees), the step down may scrape the opponent's shin and may stomp or crush the opponent's feet.

76

Eighteen Buddha Hands

Footwork

Circle Step

Technique: 1) Hands akimbo or chambered in a right horse stance. In one smooth motion: 2) Draw the right foot back and in a semi-circle, coming ankle to ankle, skim the ground with the toes and move forward six inches, bring up the back foot heel-to-toe on line, returning to the right horse. 3) Center, sink, and root before stepping again.

Changes: Train left, right, then alternating left and right steps in one place. Then train 1, 3 and 9 steps forward with turnarounds or return steps.

Monkey and Elephant Steps

The fundamental Chop, Circle and Advance steps are trained two ways; Monkey stepping is soft, light and silent. Elephant stepping is hard, heavy and makes the strong audible sound of "bing-bong" as the front and rear foot touch down. Both methods have their use and should be trained.

Attributes: One hard step makes the sound of "bing-bong."

Defense: Area from the knee to ankle (shin) defends across the centerline from solar plexus to feet. Foot instep may hook opponent's ankle.

Offense: Hips, knees, and ankles jam against the opponent's same.

Advance Step

Technique: 1) Hands akimbo or chambered in a right horse stance. 2) Release the coiled spring power in your stance and let it propel you forward, quickly advancing six inches toward the opponent, bring up the back foot heel-to-toe on line, returning to the right horse. 3) Center, sink, and root before stepping again.

Changes: Train left, right, then alternating left and right steps in

About the Kungfu: Fundamentals

one place then train 1, 3 and 9 steps forward with turnarounds or return steps.

Attributes: Shortest distance between two points is a straight advance step. One step makes the audible sound of "bing-bong."

Defense: Quick footwork for mobility. Advance "return step" for evasive footwork.

Offense: Chasing step to press the opponent. Stepping on the opponent's feet to render him immobile.

Quick 6 Inch Steps Forward

Return Steps

Technique: Any of the fundamental Chop, Circle, Advance steps may return backward in the same fashion as they did forward. Chop step, raise the knee and place it to the rear; circle step backwards just as forward; advance step by moving the front foot backward six inches, then the back foot. Also, the back foot backward six inches, followed by the front. Make sure to center, sink, and root before moving the next step.

Changes: Return step may be trained the same as forward step; train left, right, then alternating left and right steps with 1, 3, and 9 return steps, i.e. Step forward 9 steps—return backward 9 steps.

Defense: Quick evasive footwork for mobility.

Chop, Circle, Advance as One

Technique: 1) Hands akimbo or chambered in a right horse stance. Make three right steps as one count: 2) Chop, Circle and Advance. Do not hurry but center and root between each step. 3) Center, sink, and root before stepping again and repeat

Changes: Train 3 steps left, right, then alternating left and right steps, then train 1, 3 and 9 steps forward with turnarounds or return steps. Then train right Chop, left Circle, right Advance.

Attributes: Each step makes the sound of "bing-bong."

Footwork

Defense: Area from the knee to ankle (shin) defends across the centerline from solar plexus to feet. Foot instep may hook opponent's ankle.

Offense: Hips, knees, and ankles jam against the opponent's same.

Half Steps

This trains one half of the advance step in forward, back, left and right movements. **Technique:** 1) Hands akimbo or chambered in a right horse stance. In one continuous motion: 2) Advance step three inches (short step) forward, move three inches sideways to the right by moving the right foot and adjust the left foot, three inches left by moving the right foot and then left foot, three inches back by moving right foot back and adjusting the left. Always adjust in a stable rooted stance before continuing to step. One count is four steps; forward, right, left and back. 3) Center, sink, and root before stepping again. Gradually increase speed.

Changes: Start on the left horse. Then train right, left, and alternating left and right steps. Change the sequence to any combination such as back, left, forward, right, etc.

Attributes: Steps makes the sound of "bing-bong."

Defense: Quick footwork for mobility.

Offense: Chasing step to press the opponent. Stepping on the opponent's feet to render him immobile.

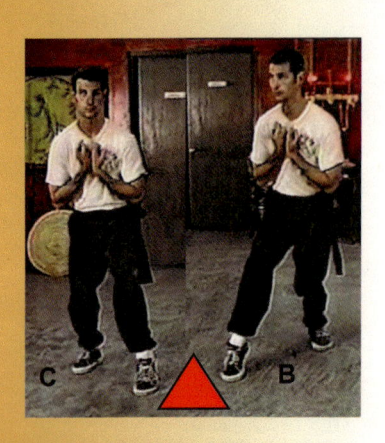

Side to Side Stepping

The late Lam Sang was skillful at this evasive footwork. Some call it "crow or raven" stepping and some call it "ghost chair" stepping. It is the ability to out flank the opponent moving swiftly side to side around him. **Technique:** 1) Hands akimbo or chambered in a right horse stance (A). In one continu-

About the Kungfu: Fundamentals

ous motion: 2) Step A1—A2 into a cat stance or empty horse on the opponent's right side (B). Step B1—B2 around to the left side of the opponent (C). In both steps one assumes a cat stance or empty front footed stance.

Changes: Opponent (red triangle) is facing you—side step to his right side, then quickly step around to his left side. Do this continuously 108 times. Start on the left horse also and repeat.
Attributes: Monkey steps are silent.
Defense: Quick footwork for mobility.
Offense: Chasing step to press the opponent. Stepping on the opponent's feet to render him immobile.

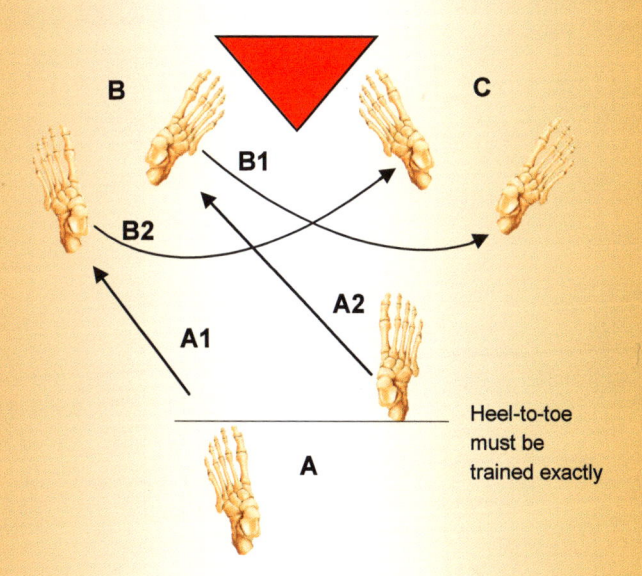

Heel-to-toe must be trained exactly

Side to Side Stepping

One Step, Two Steps, Three Steps Forward

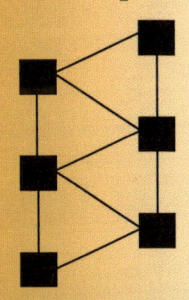

After the fundamental Chop, Circle, and Advance steps have been trained singularly with a basic degree of skill, they may be trained in tandem with a partner to develop function and distancing. Each and all three steps may be trained by stepping 1, 2, 3, or 9 steps forward and back ward. Step in unison with your partner, employing both defense and offense.

Additional Stepping Patterns

Intermediate and advanced footwork patterns may include "but are not limited" to the following:

- Diagonal Steps
- Four Corner Steps
- 180 Degree Lateral Spins
- Whole Body Ging Power
- Short Steps, Sweeps
- Leg Deflections
- Monkey Stepping
- Various Two Man Stepping

Refer to www.chinamantis.com—Instructional DVDs, Volume 9, for detailed instruction in these and other footwork patterns.

Fundamentals Continued

Once the boxing principles, posture, and fundamental footwork is understood and basically skilled, one may continue with additional fighting skills including "but not limited to"; kicks, sweeps, takedowns, grappling, chin na joint locks, hooking hands, elbow strokes, dui jong two man strengthening techniques, chi sao sticky hand, single man forms, and two man forms.

Kicking Skills

A maxim states, "You use your hands, I use my hands. You use your feet, I use my feet." Kneeing and kicking skills are primarily targeted below the waist with attacks to the toes, shins, knees, thighs, groin and tail bone. High kicks are employed to a lesser degree. Stomps are common.

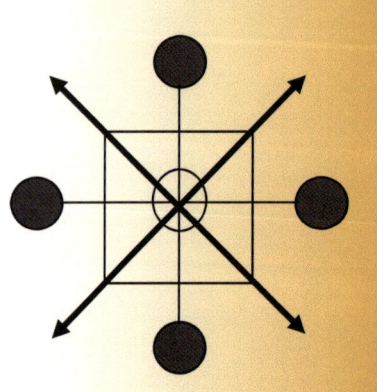

About the Kungfu: Fundamentals

Kicks may be snapped or thrust with front, crescent, side, back hook, and jump kicks taught in the two man forms.

Sweeping
Front and back foot sweeps are employed in long, short, high and low sweeping motions. These may be taught as warm-up or preliminary exercises and are trained in the two man forms.

Takedowns
The act of engaging with and purposefully taking an opponent to the ground are takedowns. They are commonly single leg sweeps taught in the two man forms.

Grappling
Techniques in which the opponent is usually held or gripped rather than struck, in order gain an advantage. Although, ground wrestling and tackling is not taught, arm bars are employed.

Chin Na Joint Locking
Gripping, seizing, grabbing, clasping, grasping are employed against the joints such as wrists and elbows. Finger claws are used to separate the soft tissue and veins and press nerve plexuses. These are taught in basic training and the two man forms.

Hooking Hands
Single and two man exercises using the inner and outer wrist joints to lock and control the opponent's arm movements. 10 hook hands is a common single man exercise and three star hook hands is a two person basic hooking method.

Elbow Strokes
10 elbow strokes is a single man exercise teaching forward, back, side elbow strikes. Sticky elbow is a two man method.

Eighteen Buddha Hands

Fundamentals, Continued

Dui Jong Two Man Strengthening
Refer to live and dead power for an understanding of natural and refined strength. Dui Jong is two man training and includes various skills such as 4 corner grinding hands and fish flops. It may be single bridge or double bridge.

Sticky Hand Training
The ability to stick to, neither pushing into or pulling away from the opponent, teaches to borrow and use force. It may be single or double bridge. Six basic methods are taught. Additionally, one may include pass offs and trapping skills simultaneously.

Single Man Forms
Form training includes, Som Bo Gin, Um Hon, 18 Point, 7 Point Fist and 108. Som Bo Gin is said to be the beginning and the end of this boxing style.

Two Man Forms
There are eight two man forms that are taught before Master's level;

- Loose Hands
- One Som Bo Gin
- Loose Hands Two
- 108 Subset
- Um Hon One
- Um Hon Two
- Mui Fa Plum Flower
- Eighteen Point
- The Master level form is 108

Dai Sihing Sibok Wong Baklim

Som Bo Gin

Three Phases of Training

Conscious Training

By daily conscious training of the 18 hands offensively and defensively in the high, middle, low, left, right, center and back gates, the mind and body will gradually come to an instinctual action and reaction based on the "partners" intent. It is too late if one must think in combat. Conscious, Instinctual, and Intuitive are the three phases one passes through.

Instinctual Training

In the beginning, one must be conscious of every minor correction before all skills become instinctual without thought. Like driving a car, one at first consciously thinks of applying the breaks, blinkers, horn, accelerator but in time one instinctually drives while adjusting the radio and talking on the phone. So it is when one reaches the instinctual level of boxing.

Intuitive Training

From Instinct, one will gradually over a long period of time, in two man training, reach the intuitive level where one can read the opponent's anticipated or telegraphed motions before he has made them. Intuitively, one will know the opponent's intent and react by instinct.

Eighteen Buddha Hand Skills

*nothing for show, everything for use,
function over form*

十八佛手

18 Empty Hands - Defense and Offense

Empty Hands are Swords, Fingers are Daggers

Buddhist compassion is antithetical to carrying weapons, but training the hands and body as a weapon of self-defense isn't. In many martial arts the term "Buddha Hand" is common. Kwongsai, Chu Gar and Iron Ox Praying Mantis all refer to empty Buddha Hands.

Before training the defensive and offensive hand skills, one must train the various two man strengthening exercises which increase one's live power. These include single and double bridge exercises such as grinding hand.

In training the 18 hands, one will do well to remember the three fundamentals of Southern Mantis boxing; rooting, feeling hand, and vital points.

Eighteen Buddha Hands

HANDS ARE A PAIR OF DOORS

Open the Doors and invite them in.

Close the Doors and send them out.

HAT YI SAO—BEGGAR'S HAND FIGHTING STANCE

18 Basic Hand Skills

This Hakka Mantis 'on guard' position is meant to entice the opponent into the Mantis door and then trap. The basic traps are contained in the Som Bo Gin single and two man forms.

There are variations in the Beggar Hand posture. It may be double bridge (hand) as in the photo left of Louie Sifu, or single bridge. One may scowl and show the teeth to ward off the opponent or appear soft and weak to entice the opponent into a trap.

Open the doors and you expose the centerline, close the doors and you protect it. Above the solar plexus is the upper gate, between it and the groin is middle gate, and below the groin is lower gate. Opening and closing the centerline gates, you use your hands, I use hands. You use your feet, I use feet. Visible fists strike invisible blows.

In the postures below, Siboks Wong and Eng show a low beggar's stance which lessens the target area for an attack. Lam Sang Sigong assumed low to the ground postures in his first generation teaching.

**1st Disciple
Dai Sihing
Wong Baklim
Circa 1950's
Lam Sang 1st Generation**

**Sibok
Jesse Eng
Circa 1950's
Lam Sang 1st Generation**

When you show your temper, hold your hand. When you show your hand, hold your temper.

Eighteen Buddha Hands

Mor Sao
Grinding Hand

- Redirect Force

- Slice Don't Bang

- Inner and Outer Hooks

Defensive Hand 1 of 9

Defensive Hands

Upper
Middle
Lower Gate

Mor Sao is the mother, the foundation, of Mantis hands. Mantis horse stance is the father of power. In circular motions, from the outside, close the doors across the centerline from the upper gate to the groin. The direction may reverse opening the doors from inside to outside. One may slam the door shut.

Attributes: Feeling, listening, turning, sticky, sensitivity, neutralize, redirect.

Function: Inside, Outside, Low, Middle, High, Single Bridge, Double Bridge.

Eighteen Buddha Hands

Gwak Shu Sweeping Hand

Mantis Hook with the Outer Wrist

Redirect Force

Slice Don't Bang

Defensive Hand 2 of 9

Defensive Hands

Middle to Lower Gate

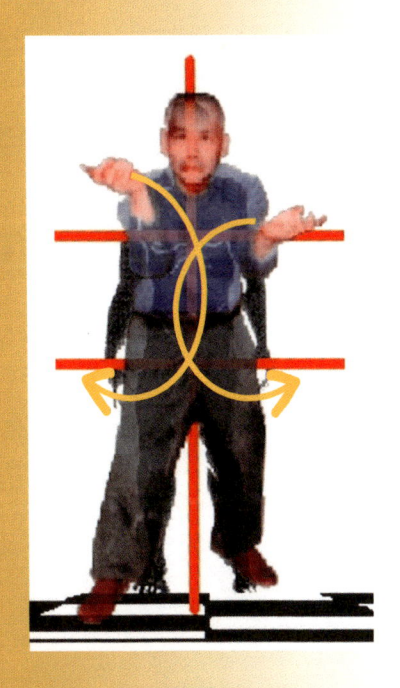

Gwak Shu, sweeping hand, as if sweeping to the side with a broom. Hook with the outer wrist across the centerline down and out from the solar plexus to the groin.

Attributes: Slicing not banging. Hook from the forearm and slice back to the wrist.

Function: Inside, Outside, Low and middle gate, Single bridge, Double bridge.

Eighteen Buddha Hands

Choc Shu Open the Doors

Mantis Hook with the Inner Wrist

Redirect Force
Slice Don't Bang

Defensive Hands

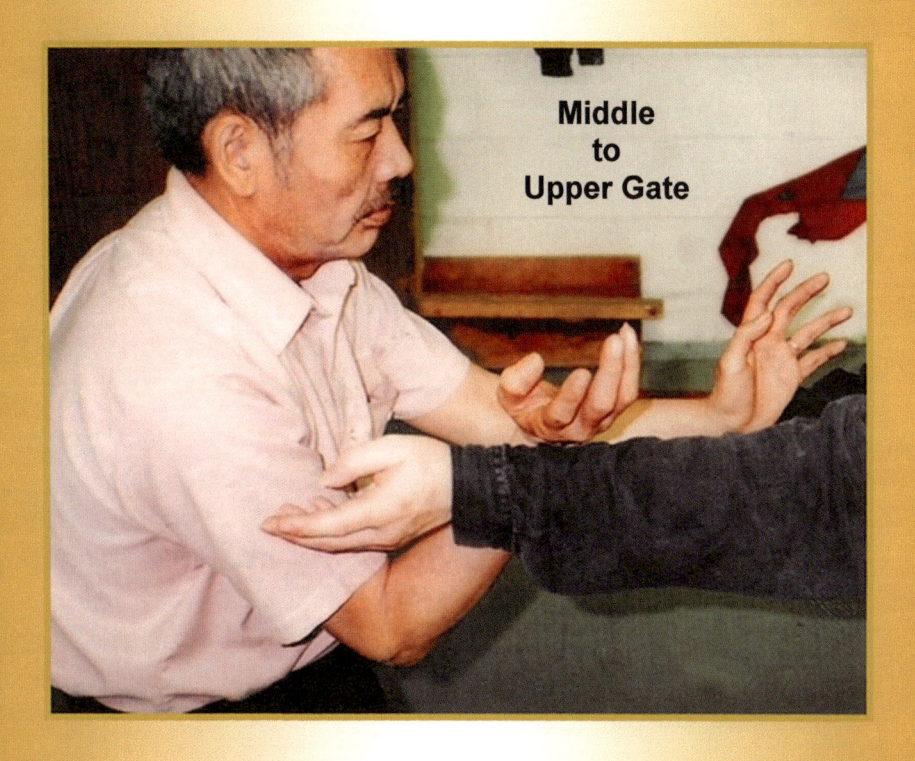

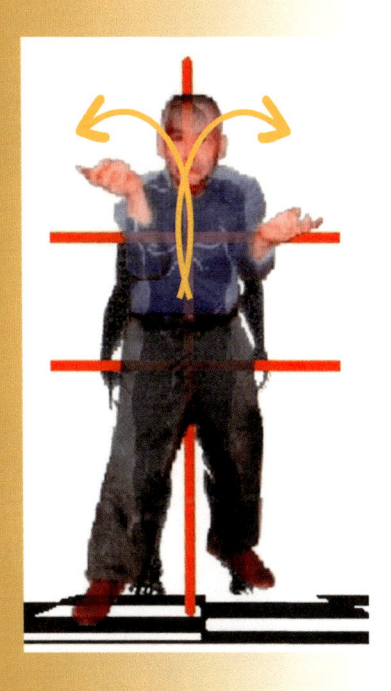

Middle to Upper Gate

Choc Shu, opens the centerline outward. Hook with the inner wrist across the centerline up and out from the solar plexus to the upper gate (head).

Attributes: Slicing not banging. Hook from the forearm and slice back to the wrist.

Function: Centerline defense, Inside, Outside, Upper and middle gate, Single bridge, Double bridge.

Eighteen Buddha Hands

SAI SHU ROLLER ARM

Twisting Forearm Deflection

Redirect Force

Slice Don't Bang

Defensive Hand 4 of 9

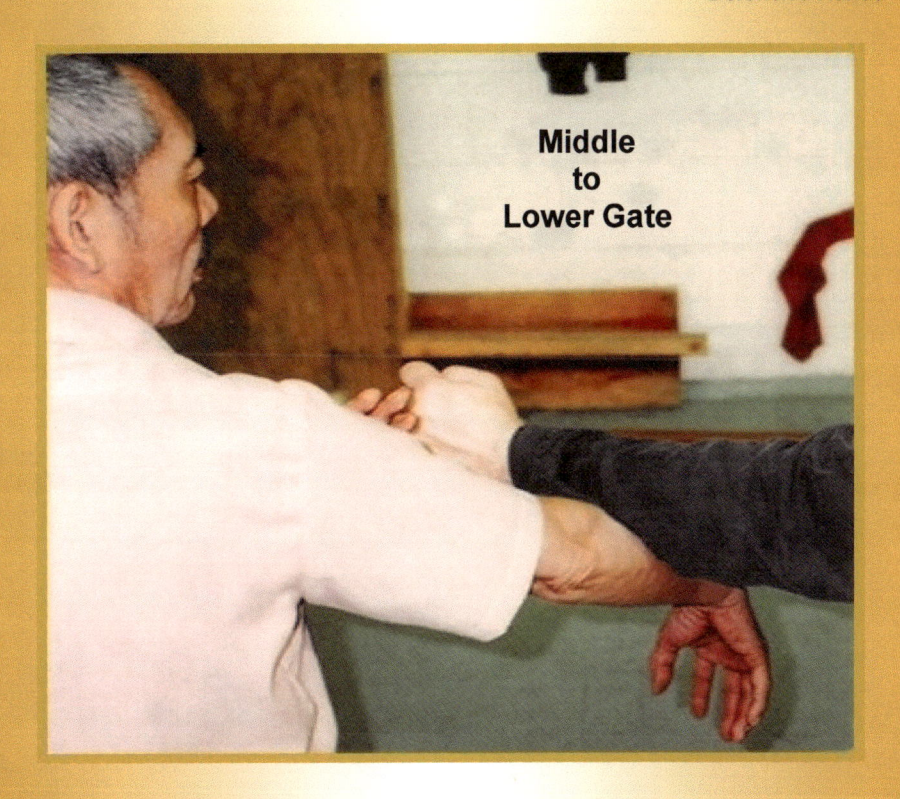

Defensive Hands

Middle to Lower Gate

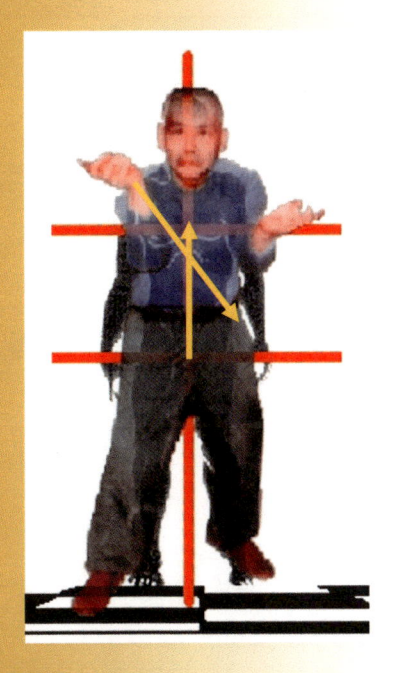

Sai Shu, a twisting forearm deflection across the centerline from middle to lower gate. Similar to Bong Sao in Wing Chun. Also used as a simultaneous strike.

Attributes: Slice and deflect incoming force across the centerline primarily from outside.

Function: Centerline defense, Primarily outside, Lower and middle gate, Primarily single bridge.

96

Eighteen Buddha Hands

Sic Shu Eating Hands

Mantis Hooks with the Outer Wrist

Redirect Force

Slice Don't Bang

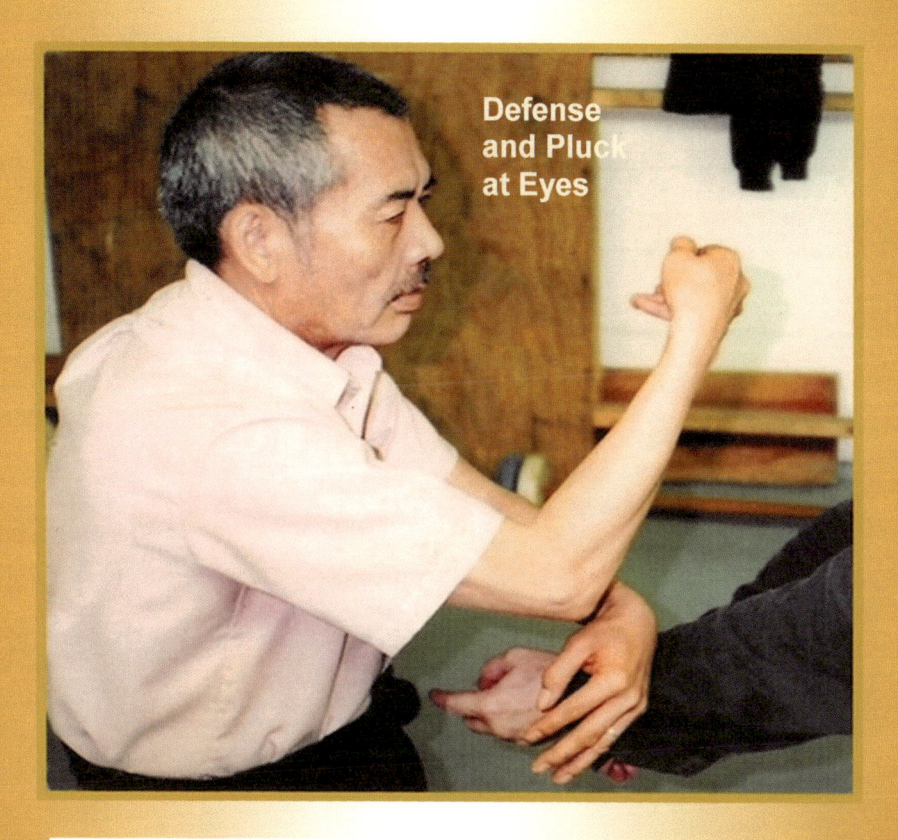

Defensive Hands

Defense and Pluck at Eyes

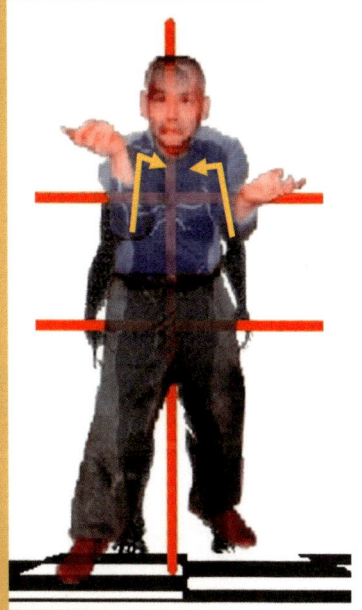

Sic Shu, eating hand, as if bringing to the mouth to eat. Slicing the forearm across the centerline from out to inside while attacking with the fingertips.

Attributes: Slice and deflect incoming force across the centerline from outside to in.

Function: Centerline defense, Outside—Inside, Middle and upper gate, Single and Double bridge.

98

Eighteen Buddha Hands

Jik Shu
Slicing
Bridge

Over and Under Forearm Slicing

Redirect Force

Slice Don't Bang

Defensive Hand

Defensive Hands

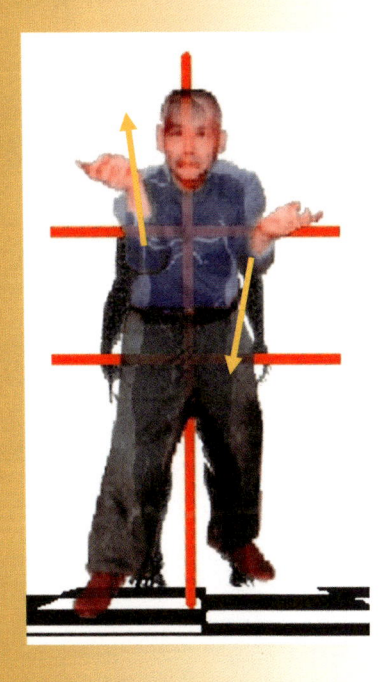

Over-Under
Upper, Mid, Lower

Jik Shu, slicing bridge, is a simultaneous forearm defense (as an ice skate blade is slicing) over or under the opponent's attack while simultaneously striking with fingertips.

Attributes: Slice and deflect incoming force across the centerline from outside to in or inside to out.

Function: Centerline defense, Outside—Inside, Middle and upper gate, Single and Double bridge. Slice through the opponent's bridge over or under.

Eighteen Buddha Hands

Spring Power Attack and Defense

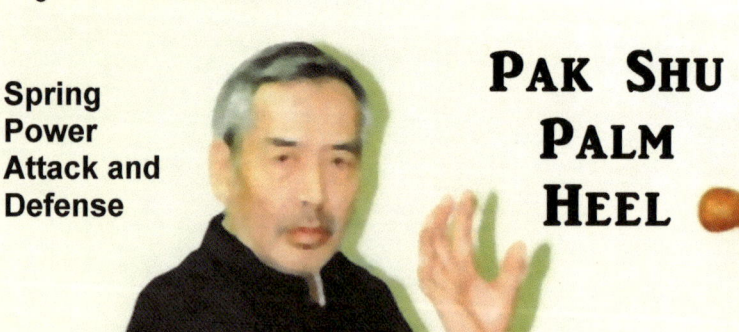

Pak Shu Palm Heel

Target: Hyper-extend the elbow

Inside and Outside Gates

Defensive Hand 7 of 9

Defensive Hands

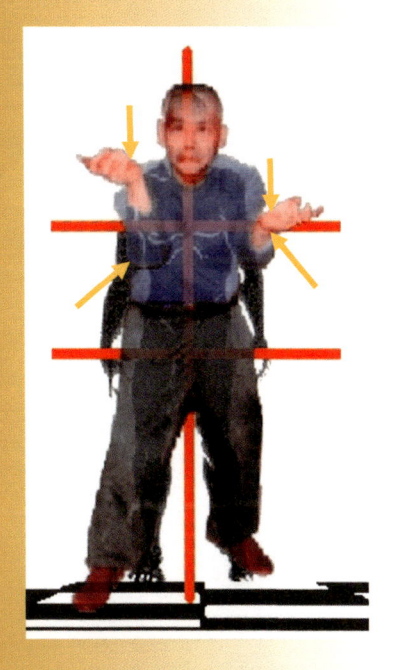

Spring Power
Snap and Thrust

Target Joints
and Cartilage

Pak Shu, a palm heel strike or deflection with spring power (ging).

Attributes: Strike or deflect incoming force across the centerline from outside to inside or inside to out.

Function: Outside—Inside, Upper, middle and lower gate, Single and double bridge. Spring power "snap" strikes to joints such as wrists and elbows and "thrust" attacks to nose, face, ribs, abdomen and kidneys with palm heel.

Eighteen Buddha Hands

Lop Shu Grabbing Hands

Mantis
Claw
Grasping
Skills

Redirect
Force

Defensive Hand 8 of 9

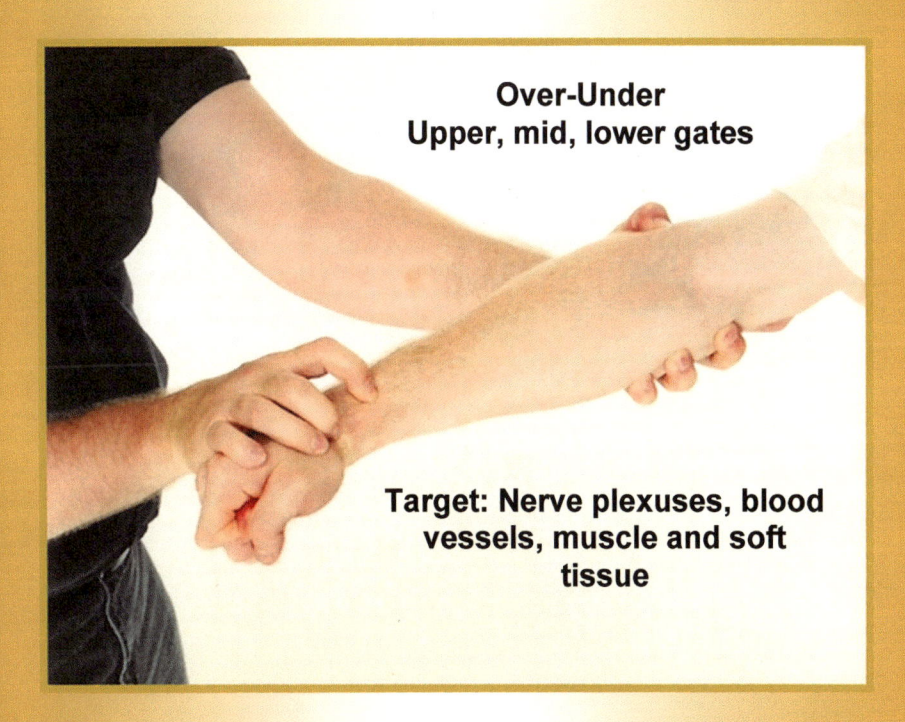

Defensive Hands

**Over-Under
Upper, mid, lower gates**

Target: Nerve plexuses, blood vessels, muscle and soft tissue

The hand going out never misses the target, the hand coming back always brings something with it (off the opponent).

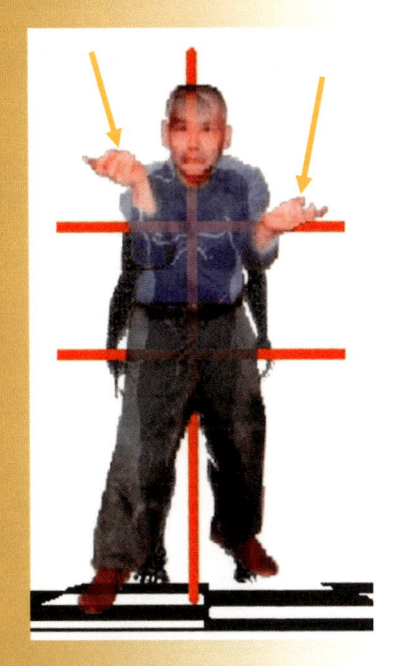

Lop Shu, grabbing hands use mantis claws to grasp nerve plexuses, blood vessels, muscle and soft tissue, such as those located at the wrists and elbows.

Attributes: Grabs may be from outside to in or inside to out.

Function: Centerline defense, Outside—Inside, Low, middle and upper gate, Single and Double bridge. This includes multiple methods of 'Chin Na' grasping using the Mantis claw skills.

Eighteen Buddha Hands

Gop Shu Clasping Hands

Short power attacks with Phoenix Eye fists

Pull off Centerline not into yourself

Defensive Hand

Defensive Hands

**Capture or close
like a vice or clasp
Basic to Mantis trapping skill**

**Single or Double
Bridge Technique**

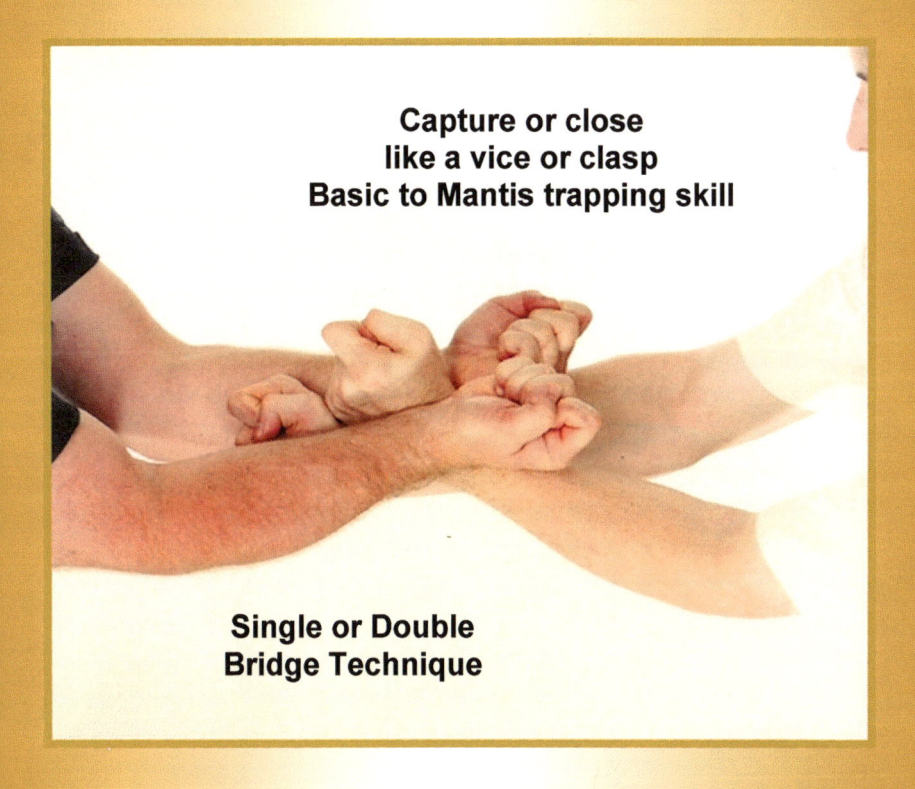

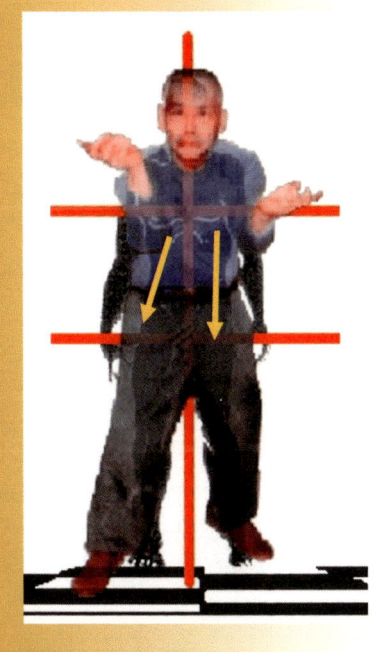

Gop Shu, clasping hands, are used for capturing and closing with the forearms in a clasp or vice, followed by short power strikes (duan ging).

Attributes: Double bridge clasps are from outside to in; single bridge may be inside or outside the centerline gate.

Function: Centerline defense, Outside—Inside, Middle gate—Double Bridge, Mid and upper gate—single bridge. Don't not pull into centerline but slightly off left or right of centerline.

Eighteen Buddha Hands
Jek Shu—Straight Strike

Short power attacks with Phoenix Eye fists

Fists attack changing angle and direction without recoil

Offensive Hands

Fist Eye Phoenix

Jek Shu, straight phoenix eye punch from chambered hands over the heart.

- Forearms and elbows protect the centerline and torso.
- Continuous inch power strikes, one following the other without withdrawing the hand, are standard (duan ging).
- The shortest distance between two points is a straight line. Hence, the quickest attack.
- Straight in attack, circular in defense is the rule.
- Attack hard, defend softly.
- Strike straight to any angle or point (108).

Solo Training: Although, Southern Praying Mantis is only mastered by two man (paired) training, the essential skills must be thoroughly trained and made one's own through solo training.

Eighteen Buddha Hands

BAO ZHANG PALM STRIKES

Close the doors

Palms against hard targets

Fists attack soft targets

Attack Sequence: Jek Shu Bao Zhang

Offensive Hands

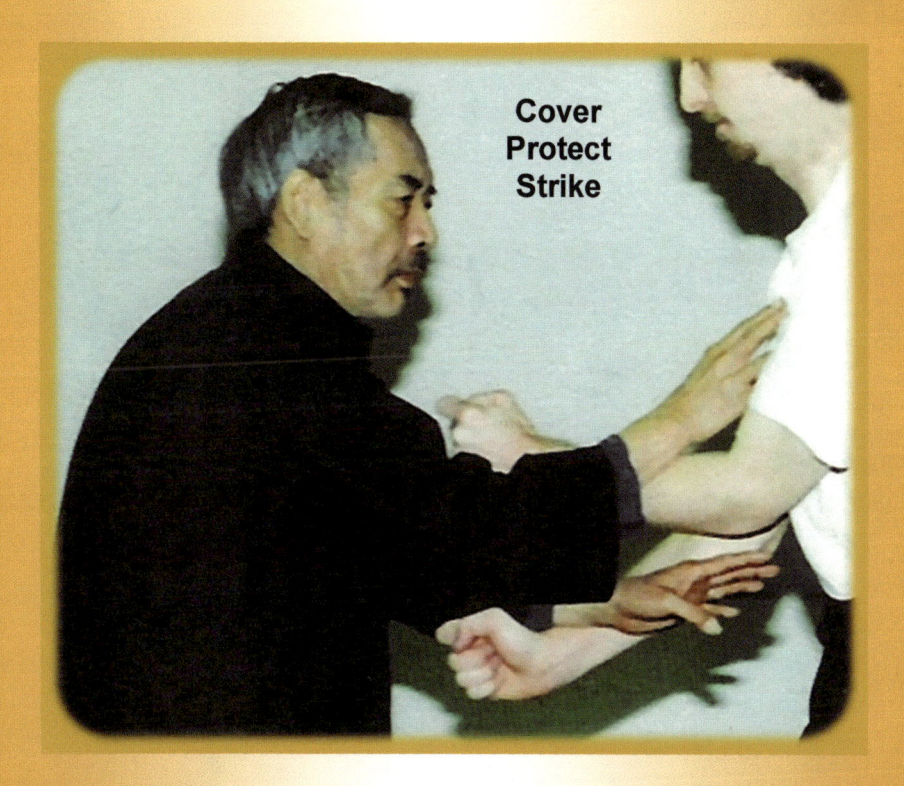

Cover Protect Strike

Bao Zhang, palm skills are sometimes defense or offense and sometimes defense and offense together, as above.

- Palms cover, bind, protect, defend, shield and palm strike.
- Palm attacks sometimes preceded by fingertip strikes which flatten into palm strikes.
- Against soft targets use fists.
- Against hard targets strike with the palms.
- From beggar's hand, slam the doors shut and palm strike.

Solo Training: One must set a personal schedule and train himself daily until the fundamental footwork, 18 hand skills, single man forms, two man forms, apparatus, and weapons are instinctually understood.

Eighteen Buddha Hands

Bil Jee Exploding Fingers

Poke
Rake
Slice
Grab

Target:
Eyes
Throat
Underarms

Attack Sequence:
Jek Shu
Bao Zhang
Bil Jee

Offensive Hands

Fingertips attack soft tissue

Simultaneous defense and offense

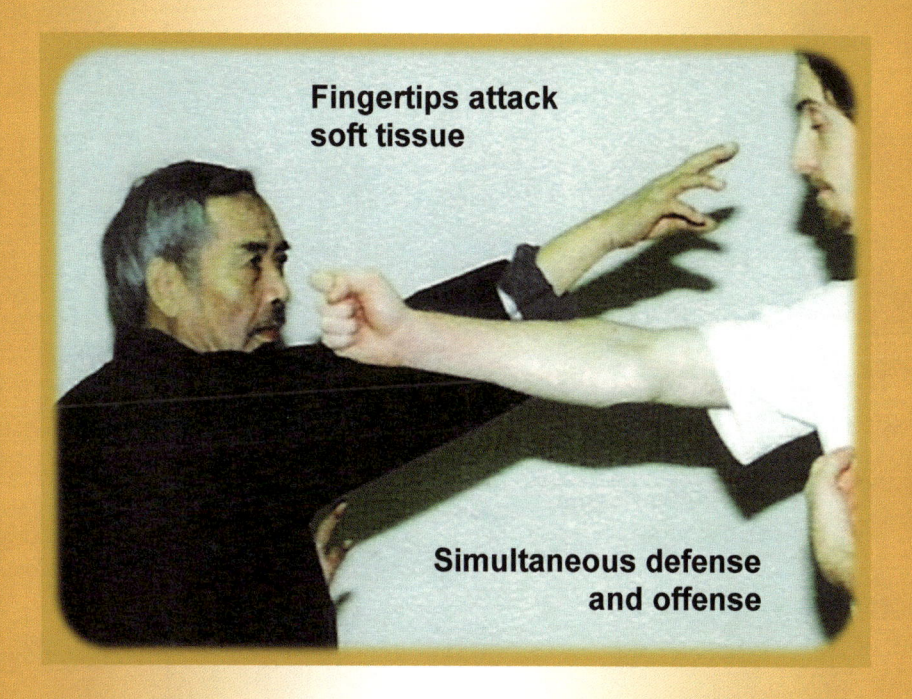

Bil Jee, exploding fingers from the fists; this skill is a fundamental of Southern Praying Mantis.

- Poke, rake, slice and grab.
- Chop and flicking actions with the fingers.
- Fingertip strikes followed by Mantis clawing actions.
- Attack sequence, Jek Shu, Bao Zhang, Bil Jee; three continuous strikes. Bil Jee can be defense and offense in one motion.
- Jek Shu straight fist strike followed by finger pokes without recoiling the arm.

Paired Training: Self-defense requires two man training to be realistic and cannot be learned by shadowboxing alone. A crude maxim states, "one must borrow another's hand, but never hang his meat on their hook." This means you must borrow the opponent's force to use against him, but never give him your force to use against you.

Eighteen Buddha Hands

PING SHU FLICKING FINGERS

Poke
Rake
Slice
Grab

Target:
Eyes
Ears
Neck
Biceps
Abdomen
Groin

Attack Sequence:
Jek Shu
Bao Zhang
Bil Jee
Ping Shu

Offensive Hands

Simultaneous defense and offense

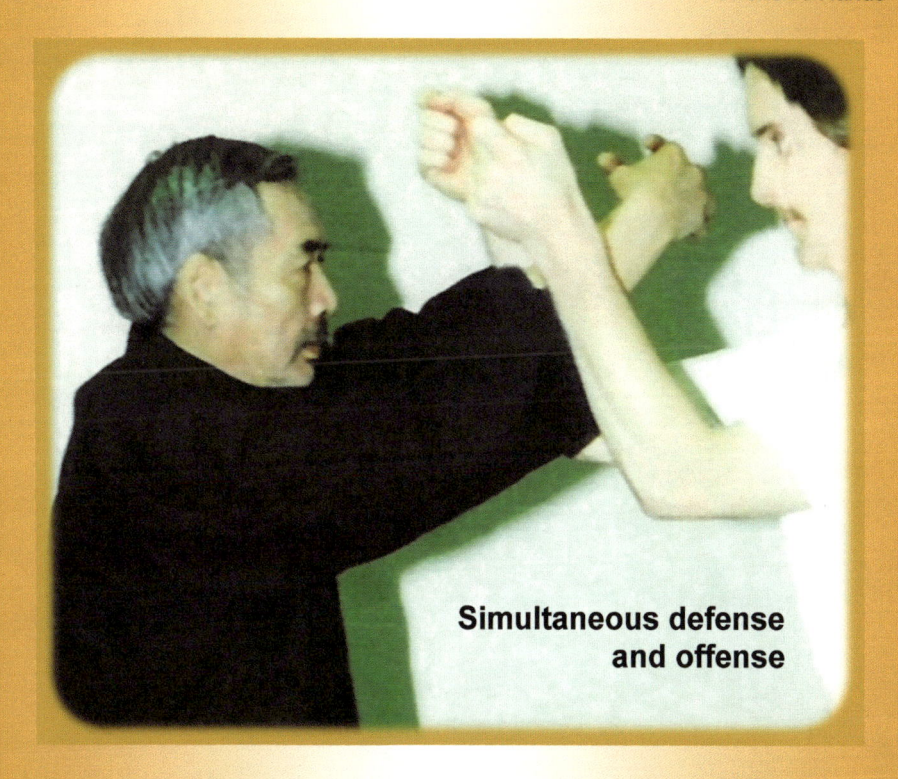

Ping Shu, includes flicks with the fingertips to soft tissue targets and strikes with the backs of the hands. Sometimes called "Fic Shu".

- Simultaneous forearm defense and attack with backs of the hands or fingertip flicks in snapping and whip actions.
- Single or double bridge; Inside or outside the bridge.
- Attack sequence—from Bil Jee immediately flick with fingertips without recoiling.

Paired Training: Two man training includes but is not limited to conditioning, strengthening, stepping—basic one, three and nine steps forward and back, sticky hands, sticky legs, sticky body, two man forms and vital point target practice. Additionally, two man apparatus and long and short weapons may be trained for further refinement of condition, strength, and skill.

Eighteen Buddha Hands

Jung Shu Uppercuts

Fingertips
Phoneix Eye
Dragon Fist

Target:
Under the Chin,
Throat
Underarms
Abdomen

Attack Sequence:
Jek Shu
Bao Zhang
Bil Jee
Ping Shu
Jung Shu

Offensive Hands

Simultaneous defense and offense

Jung Shu, uppercut strikes, some not unlike western boxing, which may include use of the fingers, phoenix eye fist (index finger knuckle) and dragon fist (middle finger knuckle) for attack.

- Defend with one hand, attack uppercut with the other.
- Simultaneous forearm defense (second hand) and uppercut attack (first hand) in one motion.
- Single or double bridge; Inside or outside the bridge.
- Attack sequence—from a Ping Shu strike, immediately change hands and strike with the opposite hand an uppercut.

Without Mistake: Give yourself up to follow others and your hand will accurately weigh their force and your feet will measure the distance of their approach without mistake. That is, root, use listening hand and stick with the opponent borrowing his force.

Eighteen Buddha Hands

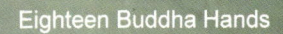

Chop Shu Finger Pokes

Target:
Neck
Clavicle
Carotid Artery

Attack Sequence:
Jek Shu
Bao Zhang
Bil Jee
Ping Shu
Jung Shu
Chop Shu

Offensive Hands

Simultaneous defense and offense

Chop Shu, finger pokes—one, two, three and five finger strikes to the neck, clavicle and carotid artery.

- Over (above photo) and under the opponent's bridge.
- Simultaneous forearm defense (second hand) and finger poke attack (first hand) in one motion.
- Single or double bridge; Inside or outside the bridge.
- Attack sequence—from a Jung Shu uppercut, immediately without recoil, strike Chop Shu with the same hand.

Leverage and Positioning: To stick means to yield to the opponent's force. If he strikes with 100% power I may use 99% of my power to turn his power against him. Or I may use 10% if the timing and position is correct. An ounce may turn a thousand pounds if the leverage is correct.

Eighteen Buddha Hands

Gow Choy Hammer Fist

Target:
Head
Solar Plexus
Eyes
Temples

Attack Sequence:
Jek Shu
Bao Zhang
Bil Jee
Ping Shu
Jung Shu
Chop Shu
Gow Choy

Offensive Hands

Four Corners Six Directions

Gow Choy, Hammer fist is a key tool of Southern Praying Mantis. Commonly employed with "Sai Shu" turning to hammer fist in one continuous movement.

- 12-6; 3-9 attacks. (page 47)
- Above photo — Mor Sao defense, Hammer Fist over
- Primarily single bridge; Inside or outside the bridge.
- Attack sequence — over, under, inside, outside, ginger fist, pai choy — four corners, six directions using the opponent's force.

Trapping Hands: In crossing hands, use the mantis traps to control the other's arms so you may land clean strikes of your own at will.

120

Eighteen Buddha Hands

Jang Shu

Elbow Strokes

Attack Sequence:
Jek Shu
Bao Zhang
Bil Jee
Ping Shu
Jung Shu
Chop Shu
Gow Choy
Jang Shu

Target: Soft Tissue with the Elbow Tip

Offensive Hands

Segmented Power

Jang Shu, elbow strokes as defense and offense. Sticky elbow methods are many and varied and contained in the two man forms.

- 10 elbow strokes is a basic exercise; Forward, right, left, 90 degree turns, and step back footwork pattern.
- Above photo—segmented power—second hand elbow stroke turns to first hand fingertip strike.
- Continuous alternating lateral elbow strokes.
- Primarily single bridge; Inside or outside the bridge.

Offense and Defense: You can prevent your opponent from defeating you through defense, but you cannot defeat him without taking the offensive.

-Sun Tzu

Eighteen Buddha Hands

HAN SHU

SLICE
DEFLECT
ATTACK

Target:
Eyes
Ribs
Abdomen

Attack Sequence:
Jek Shu
Bao Zhang
Bil Jee
Ping Shu
Jung Shu
Chop Shu
Gow Choy
Jang Shu
Han Shu

Offensive Hands

Three Point Contact

Han Shu, slicing and attacking in three points; a forearm deflection with a simultaneous finger attack, and a lower phoenix eye, fingertip, or plam strike.

- Above photo—right outside gate.
- Primarily double bridge; Inside or outside the bridge. Primarily outside gate.
- Left, right, and center Han Shu may be employed.

Offense and Defense: Each of the 18 basic hand skills may also be trained three ways; defense only, defense and strike with the same hand, defense and strike with the opposite hand. Train left, right and alternating in various footwork patterns, solo and paired training.

Eighteen Buddha Hands

TO SUBDUE THE ENEMY WITHOUT FIGHTING IS THE HIGHEST SKILL. –SUN TZU

PRINCIPLES	DEFENSIVE	OFFENSIVE
Warrior Spirit	Mor Sao	Jek Shu
Rooting	Gwak Shu	Bao Zhang
Centering	Choc Shu	Bil Jee
Body Posture	Sai Shu	Ping Shu
Footwork	Sic Shu	Jung Shu
Ging Power	Jik Shu	Chop Shu
Fist Methods	Pak Shu	Gow Choy
Solo Training	Lop Shu	Jang Shu
Paired Training	Gop Shu	Han Shu
Vital Points		

When drinking water, one should drink as close to the source as possible, as the water becomes murky and often polluted the further down stream one travels.
...Hakka Boxing Maxim

> As we express our gratitude, we must never forget that the highest appreciation is not to utter words, but to live by them. —JFK

派 螂 螳 寺 林 竹

Acknowledgements

Special thanks, always, to my Dear Brother-Friend and Associate Publisher, Jerry Chau. Although, he has no interest in Kungfu, he embodies many of the best traits of a traditional martial artist, such as loyalty, reliability, and purpose. His life-long friendship has made my life-long Chinese martial arts journey richer and more fulfilling.

And I'll never forget too, my friendship and every Monday conversations with the late Sibok Harry Sun. He urged me onward to make Southern Praying Mantis available to you.

Sincere gratitude to Ms. Huang Yan, my daily assistant and companion, and Charles Alan "Wadsworth" Clemens, editor, for his keen eyes.

竹林寺內煉精功

三達門中傳妙手

Appendix A: Lam Sang's Three Generations

In China, it is said that Lam Sang taught Southern Praying Mantis in the 1930s in Hong Kong. And in the 40s, he taught students in Liverpool, England. Some say, his Mantis teaching in Liverpool continues to this day.

From the mid 1950s until his passing in 1991, Grandmaster Monkey, Lam Sang, taught hundreds of students in New York City, Chinatown, USA. And from those hundreds, he choose a handful of students each decade, who became by ceremony, his personal pupils. He taught them Mantis boxing and "Shen Kung", a type of spiritualism, commonly called "Spirit Boxing".

His personal disciples were given new names as initiates into his Pai (faction). They also received amulets of silver bearing the name of Kwongsai Dragon Tiger Mountain Bamboo Forest Temple (shown below).

At the Hip Sing Tong, Chinese merchant Association, in the mid 1950s, Lam accepted eight personal disciples and they sometimes

Appendix A: Lam Sang's Pai

lived together in one apartment. Refer to page eleven for a group photo of the Association and its student body. The photograph below shows several of his first generation personal disciples from that period. Some were unavailable for the picture.

Circa 1963, Lam Sang was persuaded to leave the Hip Sing Association and become the Kungfu master of the Chinese Freemason Association, which was a thriving fraternity of like-minded peo-

Lam Sang's First Generation, Circa 1958
Clockwise from bottom right: Dai Sihing (1st Disciple) Wong Baklim, The Lam Sang Sifu, Ah Leung, Ah Hing, and late Sibok Harry Sun.

ple with roots going back to 1700 and memberships worldwide. From the student body there, he accepted another clique of seven personal disciples. Several of these second generations went on to teach others. Particularly, Master Gin Foon Mark's promotions over the decades have made Kwongsai Jook Lum Temple Mantis popular worldwide. The below photograph is Lam Sang's second generation disciples. Although, Louie Jack Man had made two personal disciple ceremonies to Lam Sang, one to learn Mantis and one to learn spiritualism, he was unavailable the day this photo was taken.

Lam Sang's Second Generation, Circa 1968
Clockwise from bottom right: Late Chen Ho Dun, The late Lam Sang Sifu, Gin Foon Mark, Lee Boa, Chuk Chin, Ng Sho.

After returning to the USA in 1981, Lam Sang also accepted a third generation of five disciples. He passed in 1991, of old age.

Author's Note: A note of respect to all brothers, students, and disciples of Lam Sang and the Bamboo Forest Temple Mantis worldwide, that I have not herein detailed further.

Lam Sang seated right of the Lion. Among many esteemed Mantis brothers are Wong Baklim and Harry Sun from the first generation and Chen Ho Dun, Gin Foon Mark and Louie Jack Man of the second generation, circa 1963.

130

1963. Lam Sang seated right of the Lion. Kan Tak Hing (Wong Fei Hong movie star) 2nd left of Lion. Included are Wong Baklim from the first generation and Chen Ho Dun, Gin Foon Mark, Louie Jack Man, and Henry Wong of the second generation.

1965. Hung Mun Sports Association. Esteemed brothers include Chen Ho Dun and Chuck Chin among many others

一九六五年 紐約洪門專青年會春節拜圍師彭記念

Eighteen Buddha Hands

Three Generations—One Teaching

Although, Lam Sang taught Southern Praying Mantis for some forty years in the USA and had three generations of "inner and outer gate" students, his teaching has remained constant. The Art is much the same as it was when Lam Sang planted the seed nearly six decades ago.

In the early 1960s, Lam Sang's first student to make the disciple ceremony, Sibok Wong Baklim, founded the Bamboo Temple Chinese Benevolent Association in order to preserve and promote the Mantis teaching of Lam Sang. The announcement was featured in the local Chinatown newspapers and Chinese media. Today, we continue to carry forward this legacy some sixty years later. You can join a Bamboo Temple study group or school in several locations internationally (page 148).

Members of our Association do not practice martial art for self-aggrandizement, tournaments or competitions. Our Art is not a sport. Our training is aimed toward developing supportive skills and habits which can be used in daily life. Our practice is of an inner nature and therefore we don't boast or commercialize ourselves or our martial art.

Anecdote: In the late 1950s and early 60s, Lam Sang's Mantids were well known in NYC. They all wore jackets with the Mantis emblem and when occasion required they enforced the law. One such occasion, some sailors on shore leave had come to Chinatown in search of fun and pleasure, and on a main street accosted a Chinese girl. Perhaps they didn't mean any serious harm but were obviously harassing the maiden. To the sailors dismay, Lam Sang's Mantids who patrolled that section of Chinatown happened upon the scene and quickly rendered the aggressive sailors harmless, leaving them disabled on the sidewalk. The maiden escaped without giving thanks to her benefactors and the Mantids never asked for any.

We believe men must have honor and live in love, faith, hope, goodness, kindness, generosity, and peace.

Appendix B: Miscellanies

Note on Hand Names and Translations

Many of Lam Sang's students came from Taishan, Guangdong, China. Everyone has their own "jia xiang hua", or home town dialect in China and the Taishan (Toisan) dialect has influenced the names used in reference to Lam Sang's Mantis teaching today.

It is said that Lam Sang didn't have names for the individual skills early on. It was his disciples, in an effort to remember each skill, that gave common names to each technique. An example is Lam's Qigong teaching, where they gave names like, "shoot a basketball" and "hold a ball".

The names given herein to the 18 Buddha Hands are the names that were most commonly used so that everyone was on the same page and understood which skill or hand was being talked about. It is less important what you call the skills, and more important that everyone understands.

The Chinese romanization herein is the same—it is written phonetically or what is common, so that it can be easily understood. Chinese names herein are not correct pinyin, purposely.

"Shu, Sao, and Shou" all simply mean "hand" and are often used interchangeably. Remember, once the stance, root and feeling hand is skilled, the whole body is one "hand".

About Southern Mantis on the Internet

The internet and DVDs can be a great aid to learning. How much better are DVDs than secretly peaking through holes in a fence or wall to learn Mantis? In the early days, sneaking a peek through a hole was

Appendix B: Miscellanies

quite common. Wong Yuk Kong was said to have started his training under Chung Yel Chong by watching through a hole in the wall. How much better to have YouTube or a DVD that you can fast forward, rewind or play in slow motion!

Nothing can replace the spirit and hand of a skillful teacher. But, the new media and resources are still a valuable asset.

The internet, however, is also a large source of disinformation. Repeating what someone else said erroneously, often becomes accepted as SPM "truth", without verification. There is a great deal of "false" information on the internet about Southern Praying Mantis.

An example is the 'Blanco' article. Circa mid 1990s, Blanco, from Hong Kong, called my office in the USA asking how to contact Southern Mantis teachers in China. I wasn't able to provide him any information. Southern Mantis teachers usually frown on unannounced visits from strangers. Later, he "compiled" his article using sources, such as my published works, without permission. Much of his article is erroneous and needs correction.

I encourage you to seek the truth for yourself. Do not follow any one blindly. Search and prove all things. The further you go downstream the murkier the water. Drink close to the source.

About the Photographs in this Book

The images are from my personal library. They were not made in a studio for glamor, but made on the spot with the various Teachers herein. Appreciate the images for what they are - natural shots of Sifu, in their own elements. None of the images can be made again—those days are gone. Sadly, many of the elder teachers have passed away, as well.

Appendix C: Chronology

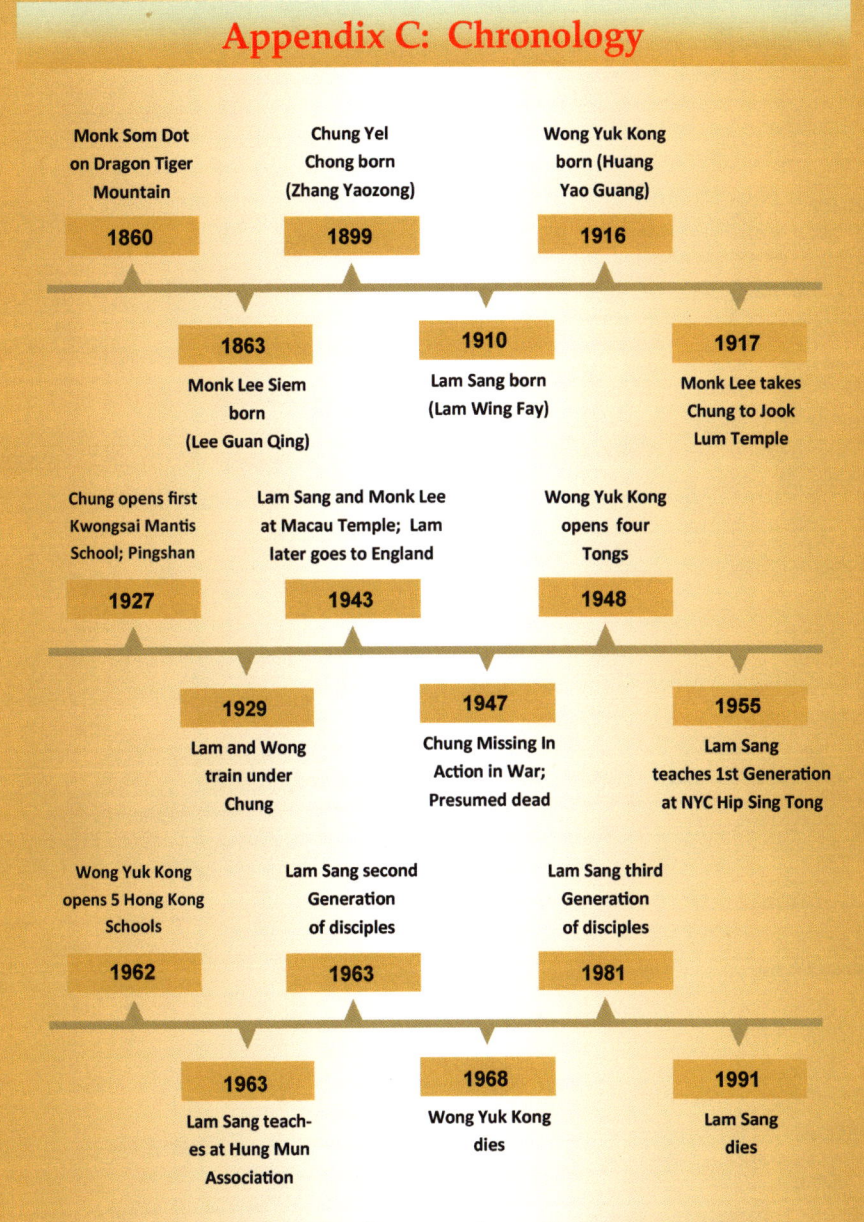

1860 — Monk Som Dot on Dragon Tiger Mountain

1863 — Monk Lee Siem born (Lee Guan Qing)

1899 — Chung Yel Chong born (Zhang Yaozong)

1910 — Lam Sang born (Lam Wing Fay)

1916 — Wong Yuk Kong born (Huang Yao Guang)

1917 — Monk Lee takes Chung to Jook Lum Temple

1927 — Chung opens first Kwongsai Mantis School; Pingshan

1929 — Lam and Wong train under Chung

1943 — Lam Sang and Monk Lee at Macau Temple; Lam later goes to England

1947 — Chung Missing In Action in War; Presumed dead

1948 — Wong Yuk Kong opens four Tongs

1955 — Lam Sang teaches 1st Generation at NYC Hip Sing Tong

1962 — Wong Yuk Kong opens 5 Hong Kong Schools

1963 — Lam Sang second Generation of disciples

1963 — Lam Sang teaches at Hung Mun Association

1968 — Wong Yuk Kong dies

1981 — Lam Sang third Generation of disciples

1991 — Lam Sang dies

All dates on this timeline are circa. It does not include all major events or any pivotal events.

Resources

Volume 1: Pingshan Mantis Celebration

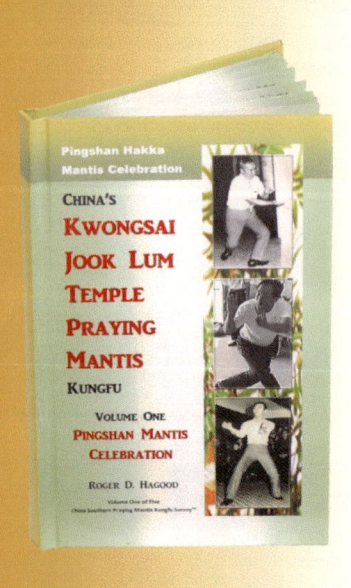

**Hardcover Book
or
eBook Available Now!**

www.chinamantis.com

In Volume One:

The 35th anniversary celebration of Wong Yuk Kong's Kwongsai Jook Lum Temple Praying Mantis heritage in Pingshan, the hometown of China's Kwongsai Mantis.

Hundreds of people, Hakka Unicorn dancing and dozens of Southern Praying Mantis demonstrations.

Demonstrations of Mantis Forms such as Single Arm, 3 Step Forward, Four Gates and many Two man weapons sets! Read China's "written history" of "Southern Praying Mantis" and hear the oral traditions.

Get your copy today!

Volume 2: China Mantis Reunion

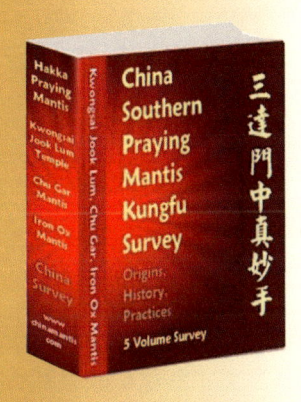

Hardcover Book
or
eBook Available Now!

www.chinamantis.com

In Volume Two:

At the request of Sifu Wong Yu Hua, a number of junior, senior and elder Southern Mantis masters, dating back to circa 1920s, gathered in Huizhou, Guangdong. It's about an hour's drive from Pingshan Town and most of the mantis brothers there had not seen each other for many years.

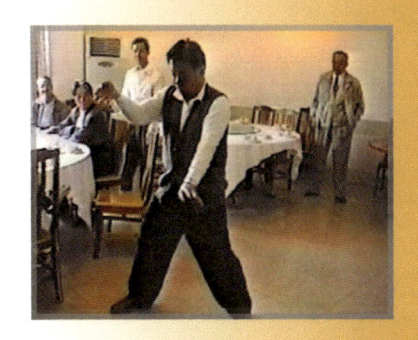

The gathering included those who in the 1930s and 40s, were among the in-crowd of Chu Gar and Iron Ox, as well as, Kwongsai Mantis. Some had studied all three branches of Som Dot's teaching. Learn directly from them and see their demonstrations of boxing and staff play in Volume Two of the China Southern Praying Mantis Survey.

Get your copy today!

Resources

Volume 3: Iron Ox / Kwongsai Mantis Interviews

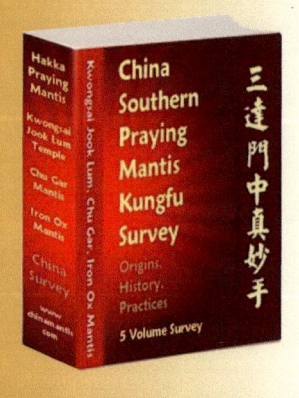

Hardcover Book
or
eBook Available Now!

www.chinamantis.com

In Volume Three:

Learn from Kwongsai Elder Master, Yao Kam Fat, who visited Lao Sui with Wong Yuk Kong. Watch his demonstrations of Third Door, Push Hands, and Plum Flower Pole Form. Hear stories which shed a great deal of light on Chung Yel Chong and Lao Sui's relationship, and other mantis ancestors.

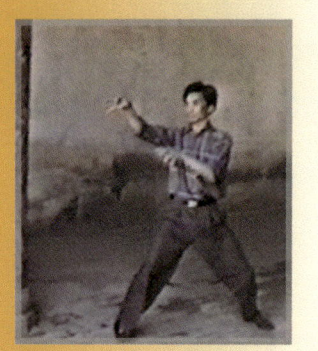

Also, Iron Uncle Chung sheds light on mantis in the very earliest days, circa 1920s.

Yang Gun Ming's family interview shows the degree that mantis once permeated south China villages.

And you will discover the origin of China's Iron Ox Praying Mantis and visit with an inheritor, Sifu Xu Men Fei, as he takes you on a tour of Pingdi, an Iron Ox Village and its ancient Clan Temple. Watch demonstrations of the Iron Ox forms Second Door, Third Door, and Big Red Pole forms! Get your copy today.

139

China Southern Praying Mantis Kungfu Survey™

Volume 4: On Som Dot's Trail / Chung Family Interviews

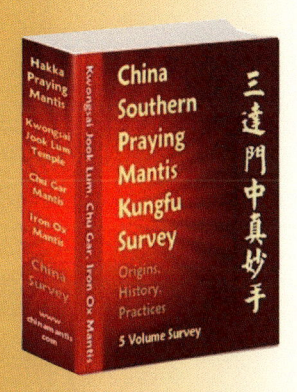

Hardcover Book
or
eBook Available Now!

www.chinamantis.com

In Volume Four:

INTERVIEWS
Visit Chung Yel Chong's (Zhang Yaozong), third ancestor's, family and clinic and watch his grandson perform treatments; an in-depth interview of Chung Yel Chong's family. Rare photographs.

An interview with Sifu Lee Kwok Liang in Hong Kong, who was a student of Kwongsai Mantis Masters Chang Gun Hoi and Wong Yuk Kong. Lee Sifu still teaches in Hong Kong today and his son, Patrick is a mantis Sifu, as well.

ON SOM DOT'S TRAIL
Visit Shanxi in the North and Jiangxi (Kwongsai) in the South of China where Som Dot and Lee Siem Yuen treaded. See what the old Bamboo Forest Temple located in Shanxi looks like today! And visit the bamboo forests of Mt. Dragon Tiger and the mansions of the first Taoist Pope where the "108" Demons were confined into a well.

Hear what the elders at the Macau Bamboo Forest Temple had to say about Lee Siem Yuen! And more. Get your copy today!

Resources

Volume 5: Chu Gar Mantis
Cheng Wan Sifu Celebrations

Hardcover Book
or
eBook Available Now!

www.chinamantis.com

In Volume Five:

You will discover more about the origins, history and practices of Chu Gar Praying Mantis.

I studied Chu Gar Mantis with Sifu Gene Chen, who was a disciple of Dong Yat Long, who was a disciple of Sun Chu Hing, who was a disciple of Lao Sui. I did "make the ceremony" of offering tea to Chen Sifu and so became his disciple in Chu Gar Mantis, circa 1989. I am also a disciple by Ceremony of the Late Grandmaster Cheng Wan in Hong Kong!

See performances of soft and hard power in Chu Gar boxing as well as learn the Origins, History and Practices of this rare Hakka Mantis boxing style.

Get your copy today!

MantisFlix™ Video eBooks

MantisFlix™ Video eBooks

60 Years of Southern Mantis Movies and Events!

Wong Fei Hong and the Jook Lum Temple

Volume 1001 - Hong Kong 1954

B/W Classic Movie Exclusive! 100,000 plus clip previews on YouTube. Get your full copy now!

Kwongsai Mantis Celebration

Volume 1002 - Pingshan Town, Guangdong, China

Late Sifu Wong Yuk Kong Kwongsai Jook Lum Clan 35th Anniversary Celebration, circa 2003.

Hakka Boxing Collection One
Volume 1003 - A rare collection of Hakka Boxing.

Hakka Boxing Collection Two
Volume 1004 - A second rare collection of Hakka Boxing.

Chu Gar Cheng Wan Celebration
Volume 1005 - Join the 1989 Cheng Wan Chu Gar Mantis Celebration in Hong Kong! Cheng Wan Sifu was the inheritor of Chu Gar descended from Lao Sui.

View and Enjoy Video Previews Online:
www.MantisFlix.com

Resources

Resources

Our Family of Hakka Mantis Websites
Visit and Enjoy! Informational, Educational, Instructive

www.SouthernMantisPress.com

A ten year ongoing research in China of the origins, history and practices of Southern Mantis! Dedicated to the late Wong Yuk Kong Sifu in China!

chinamantis.com

The Bamboo Temple Association is a mutual aid fraternity. Join us and become a member, School, Branch or Study Group today! Dedicated to the late Lam Sang Sifu's teaching in the USA.

bambootemple.com
bambootemple-chicago.com
btcba.com

These sites reveal many China Kwongsai Mantis Sifu who have heretofore remained silent about the teaching of Kwongsai Dragon Tiger Mountain Bamboo Forest Temple Mantis and outlay the lineage of Hakka Mantis as stated in China.

kwongsaimantis.com
somdotmantis.com

This site details the complete history of Chu Gar Gao Hakka Praying Mantis as descended from the late Lao Sui in Hong Kong and Hui Yang (Wai Yearn), China.

Our Family of Websites

Online

(con't) Dedicated to the late Cheng Wan Sifu who passed in 2009. chugarmantis.com

This site is dedicated to the late Xu Fat Chun Sifu and speaks of the history of Iron Ox Hakka Praying Mantis in Pingdi Town, Guangdong, China.
ironoxmantis.com

Historical Hakka Mantis Flix! Some 60+ years of Hakka Southern Praying Mantis Kungfu movies and events in video eBooks!
mantisflix.com

Our dedicated South Mantis Tube. We have several hundreds of hours of videos in our Hakka Mantis archives dating back to 1950 in China that we hope to share with you! Feel free to share. Upload your Southern Mantis or Hakka video now!
southmantis.com

Genuine Internal Work - the original 11 month correspondence course of Tien Tao Qigong.
tientaoqigong.com

Ancient Methods to achieve vitality and a healthier well-being! The Oriental Secrets Series of Qigong.
oss.tientaoqigong.com

And visit our daily YouTube feed of only Southern Praying Mantis videos!
chinamantis.com/youtube

And our YouTube channel:
youtube.com/chinamantissurvey

Resources

New Media from Southern Mantis Press.com

Southern Mantis Instructional Playing Cards

Kwongsai Mantis
18 Buddha Hands

Card Backs: Various Sifu of Lam Sang's generations in multiple postures

Card Fronts: Two man application photos, Text instruction, Instructive maxims

Includes the 18 Buddha Hands and more of Kwongsai Hakka Mantis

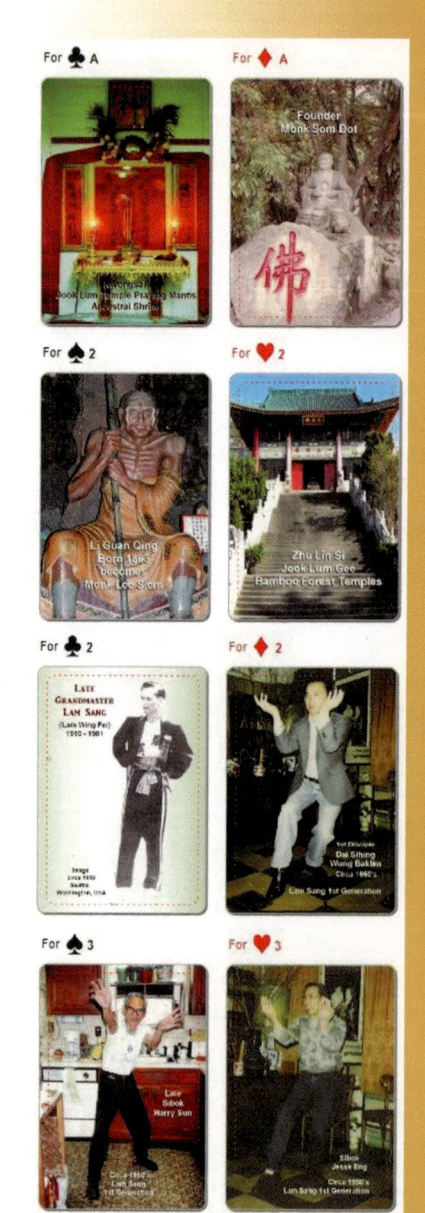

Key Benefits
of our Card Decks

- 54 Cards with Hakka Mantis
- Customized Front and Back
- Full Vibrant Color!
- Instructional
- Educational
- Informative
- Rare and Exclusive Content and Photographs
- Entertaining - Play Hakka Mantis Cards with your friends

www.SouthernMantisPress.com

Instructional Card Decks

New Media from Southern Mantis Press.com

18 Buddha Hands — Instructional Card Deck

Card Deck Use Includes

- Useful gifts for martial artists
- Instructional and Informative
- Invaluable Heirloom of Hakka Mantis Masters

Card Decks Include

- 54 card deck in standard size
- Made from 100% casino quality card stock
- Clear plastic case included

Wholesale Inquiries Welcome

Other Decks Include:

- Chu Gar Mantis - "Fundamentals"
- China Kwongsai Mantis - "Celebration"

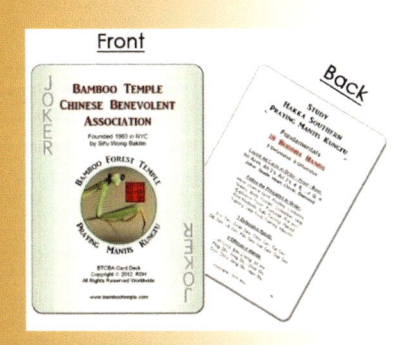

For order info email:
cards@chinamantis.com

146

Resources

ChinaMantis.com   Instructional DVDs

Jook Lum Temple Mantis Step by Step Instruction in 18 Volumes

Year One Training
Volume One: Fundamentals; The Most Important
Volume Two: Phoenix Eye Fist Attacking / Stepping
Volume Three: Centerline Defense
Volume Four: One, Three & Nine Step Attack / Defense
Volume Five: Centerline Sticky Hand Training
Volume Six: Same Hand / Opposite Hand Attacks
Volume Seven: Sai Shu, Sik Shu, Jik (Chun) Shu
Volume Eight: Gow Choy; Hammer Fist-Internal Strength
Volume Nine: Footwork in Southern Praying Mantis
Volume 10 Chi Sao Sticky Hands and Pass offs

Advanced Two Man Forms—Year Two and Three
Available by request. Prerequisite Volumes 1–10.
Volume 11: Loose Hands One
Volume 12: Som Bo Gin
Volume 13: Second Loose Hands
Volume 14: 108 Subset
Volume 15: Um Hon One
Volume 16: Um Hon Two
Volume 17: Mui Fa Plum Flower
Volume 18: Eighteen Buddha Hands
All 8 two man forms must be trained as one continuous set on both A - B sides.

Summary Year One
http://www.chinamantis.com/first-year-training.htm

Summary Year Three:
http://www.chinamantis.com/summary-of-training.htm

Join a School or Start a Study Group!

Bamboo Temple Chinese Benevolent Association

Roger D. Hagood, Standing Chairman
Hong Kong, Shenzhen, China
rdh@chinamantis.com

USA

Crystal Lake, Illinois School
Richard Lee Gamboa
USA Chief Instructor
Phone: (847) 458-2080
Mantis@ActionKungFu.com

Los Angeles, CA School
John Brown
Phone: (510) 423 1615
Tonglong108@gmail.com

Huntsville - North AL, Branch
Slade White
256-694-0949
slade@sladewhite.com

Indiana, USA Branch
Dave Marshall
812-709-0827
ictdave@aol.com

Washington DC Study Group
Eric Lewis
240-552-1338
rev_ericlewis@hotmail.com

Weslaco, TX Study Group
David Garcia
(956) 472-0254
garciads1@gmail.com

INT'L

Taipei, Taiwan Branch
Dr. Han Chih Lu
simonclh@gmail.com

London, Ontario, Canada Branch
Mike Shaw
Phone 519-852-2174
mantismike@start.ca

Düsseldorf, Germany Branch
Erik Irsch
eirsch@yahoo.de

Lima, Peru Study Group
Guillermo E. Talavera
getalavera@hotmail.com

Like minded people that have a sincere interest to study Southern Praying Mantis together and are following the Instructional DVDs may start a Study Group.
Become a group leader today!

Author's Bio

RDH Bio

Welcome to visit the Author!

Your email correspondence is welcome and do visit and study Hakka Southern Praying Mantis with me in beautiful sunny south China! I am an Author, Publisher and Producer of eBooks, books, journals, videos and 7 International martial arts newsstand magazines in 15 countries with 45 years in training and teaching martial arts and some 20 years living in China and Asia!

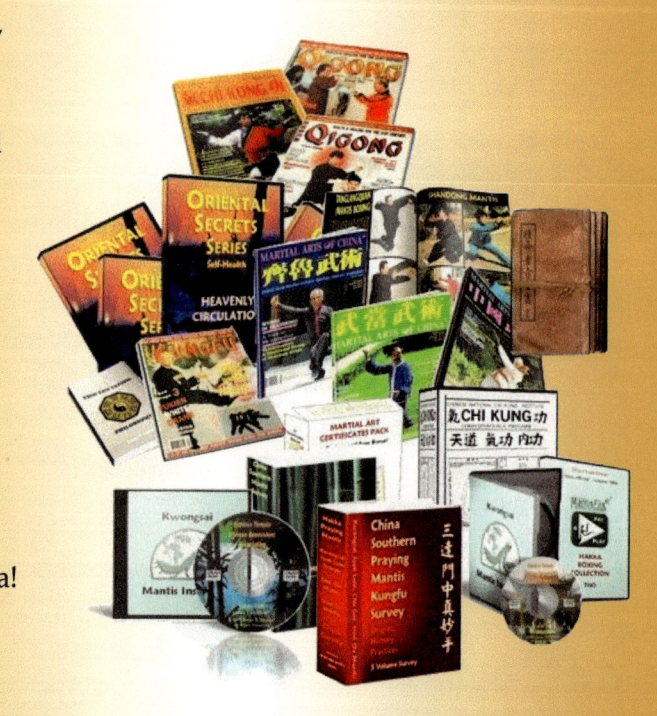

Currently residing in beautiful sunny south China for the last 10 years where I teach Southern Praying Mantis. Join my class in Guangdong today!

RDH
Pingshan Town
Summer 2012

More Bio:
http://www.chinamantis.com/roger-d.-hagood.htm
Email:
rdh@chinamantis.com

Guang Wu Tang

Study Hakka Mantis and Unicorn in China

Jook Lum Temple Mantis and Hakka Unicorn Culture

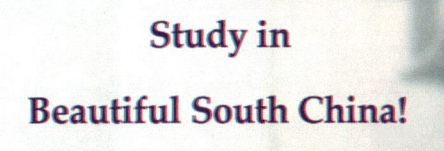

Study in

Beautiful South China!

Train Hakka Unicorn Culture at Guang Wu Tang—The Martial Hall of Wong Yuk Kong!

Sifu Wong Yu Hua
Pingshan Town
for info email:
rdh@chinamantis.com

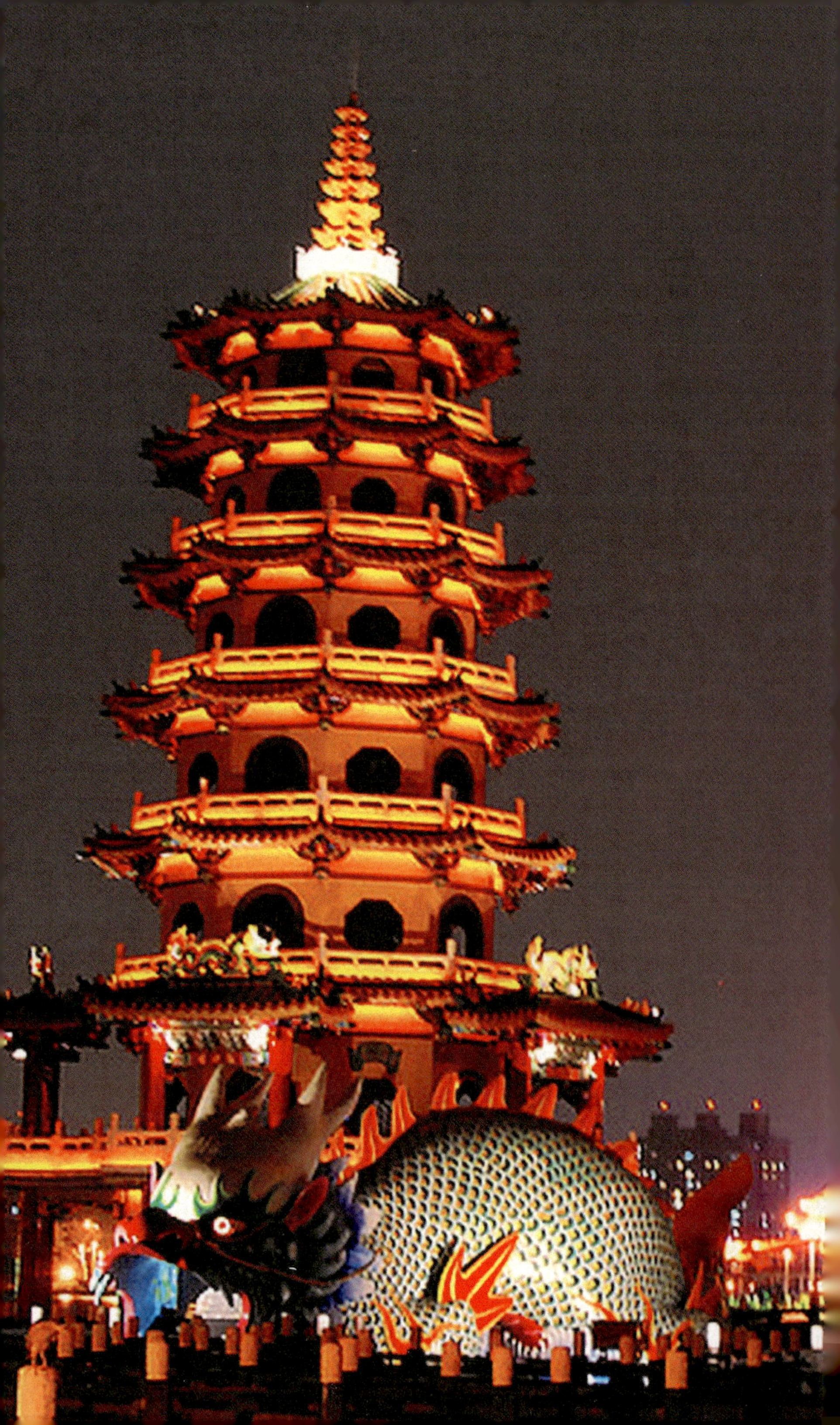